# Compliance and Financial Crime Risk in Banks

# Compliance and Financial Crime Risk in Banks: A Practitioners Guide

BY

**SOPHIA BECKETT VELEZ, PHD**

*Walden University, USA*

United Kingdom – North America – Japan – India – Malaysia – China

Emerald Publishing Limited
Emerald Publishing, Floor 5, Northspring, 21-23 Wellington Street, Leeds LS1 4DL

First edition 2024

Copyright © 2024 Sophia Beckett Velez.
Published under exclusive licence by Emerald Publishing Limited.

**Reprints and permissions service**
**Contact:** www.copyright.com

**British Library Cataloguing in Publication Data**
A catalogue record for this book is available from the British Library

ISBN: 978-1-83549-042-6 (Print)
ISBN: 978-1-83549-041-9 (Online)
ISBN: 978-1-83549-043-3 (Epub)

Printed and bound by CPI Group (UK) Ltd, Croydon, CR0 4YY

INVESTOR IN PEOPLE

*To my daughter Shikurah Velez, you are my biggest cheerleader, and I am thankful for your love and support.*
*To Victor Velez, thank you for believing in me.*
*To Peter Chidolue SJ, thank you for pushing me when I wanted to give up on my dreams.*
*To Marjorie Grant my mom whom I love so dearly, thank you for believing in my talents and investing in my education.*

# Contents

# List of Tables

**Chapter 5**

**Chapter 6**

**Chapter 7**

# About the Author

**Sophia Beckett Velez**, PhD, has worked for over 16 years as a Certified Public Accountant (CPA) with large banks providing consulting services. Her work experience has provided her with valuable background information on the banking industry in general. As a CPA, she worked for firms such as PricewaterhouseCoopers, where she performed financial audits, attestation services, and risk management analysis of large banks. Many of the regulatory compliance problems noted during her review of the large banks required her to cultivate relationships with line of business managers, and work with them to develop action plans and solutions to the issues noted. This has sparked her research interest in exploring the issues at hand in global banks.

# Preface

The US and global banking regulators have enforced regulatory compliance laws to minimize (money laundering, terrorist funding, human trafficking, fraudulent banking activities, bad mortgage loans) that exposed banks to significant risks and losses which banks have complained that it is over regulation. This book discusses anti-money laundering standards, counter-terrorist financing measures that are aligned to AML program that cover BSA laws and control activities (prevent, detect, monitor) designed to mitigate breaches.

A qualitative e-Delphi study of 10 banking finance experts were convened to build consensus on compliance practices senior bank managers can implement that can be effective in reducing losses in banks/bank holding companies. This book offers consensus on (a) maintenance of effective and independent compliance consistent with the organizational objectives, (b) clear definition of data source for compliance analytics, (c) compliance monitoring, (d) reporting activities promptly to upper management, (e) top leadership must be a champion of code of ethics, and (f) understanding regulatory compliance activities that are effective.

This book offers an original contribution to the field of banking that undergraduates, master's, PhD students, academics, and researchers can use to gain a deeper understanding of compliance and AML risks in banks and the use of effective management practices. This book will be the first to discuss consensus on effective compliance practices in banks. Sophia Beckett Velez PhD has over 16 years of experience as a Certified Public Accountant (CPA), providing consulting services to large banks.

*Sophia Velez*
0000-0002-8382-3090

# Acknowledgments

This book could not have been written without the support and encouragement of my daughter Shikurah Velez.

# Introduction

## Outline of Chapters

This book is divided into three parts. Part 1 discusses Regulatory Compliance in Domestic and Global Banks. Part 2 examines Compliance Laws and Requirements (BSA/AML). Part 3 reviews Compliance Environment and Effective Leadership Practices.

## Part 1: Regulatory Compliance in Domestic and Global Banks

This part of the book discusses regulatory compliance laws that have placed stress both financially and operationally on large global banks in the United States of America (USA) and around the world. The lack of effective compliance risk management practices to control growth of fraud and money laundering spread throughout the global economy.

## Chapter 1: Regulatory Compliance Requirement and Practices

In this chapter, I discuss increased in regulatory compliance laws that have placed stress both financially and operationally on global banks in the United States and around the world business practices. US and global banking regulators have enforced regulatory compliance laws to minimize bank risks (money laundering, terrorist funding, human trafficking, fraudulent banking activities, bad mortgage loans) that exposed them to significant losses which banks have complained that it is over regulation.

## Chapter 2: Regulatory Compliance in Global Banks

The US and global banking regulators have enforced regulatory compliance laws to minimize bank risks (money laundering, terrorist funding, human trafficking, fraudulent banking activities, bad mortgage loans) that exposed them to significant losses which banks have complained that it is over regulation. This chapter highlights penalties and punishment issued to banks and other financial institutions for being not in compliance with SAR requirements as noted in anti-money laundering laws that have been astronomical.

## Chapter 3: Compliance Requirements in BHC and International Holding Companies (IHC)

This part of the book discusses compliance costs have increased for banks, and regulators have seen an increase in their monitoring costs of these compliance regulations. An in-depth look at some of the significant increases in banks compliance costs are related to complex tracking and reporting systems to meet the enhance compliance requirements.

## Chapter 4: Compliance Failures in Global Banks

Global banks have failed to implement an effective compliance program to address regulatory requirements of AML, Basel III, and Dodd Frank 2012 Bill. Banks assigned low-risk rating to high risk countries ignoring serious money laundering risk and opted to have lax AML control, which incentivized drug cartels and money launders to use the bank as their preferred financial institution.

## Part 2: Compliance Laws and Requirements (BSA/AML)

This part of the book discusses risk of not meeting government compliance requirement referred to as compliance risk. An in-depth look at banks and financial institutions efforts to prevent themselves from being exposed to receiving penalties due to the business risk exposure of where they transact business (high risk countries, individuals, companies) that are susceptible to the risk of money laundering.

## Chapter 5: Implications of Compliance Weakness in Banks and Regulatory Penalties

This chapter discusses banks argument that they lost their competitive edge because they have been cut back on business in some countries to meet AML regulations. Banks have failed to report accurate and complete/updated information that result in them receiving penalties.

## Chapter 6: BSA AML Compliance Practices – Ineffective Practices

BSA AML requirements have intensified in recent times to counteract the significant increase in money laundering activities; such as; currency transaction reporting (CTR) thresholds, suspicious activity reporting (SAR), and responses to 9/11 'Know Your Customer (KYC) requirements. This chapter examines significant number of banks moved from manual face-to-face know your customer exercise KYC check to an automated process, which turned out to be ineffective.

## Chapter 7: Capital Requirements – Ineffective Practices

This chapter discusses capital requirements were highlighted as key risk mitigation measure that banks and SIFIs need to sustain and survive in a financial crisis. OCC made changes to risk weights of the Advanced Approach system, made updates to the market risk rule to exclude credit rating-based risk assessment, introduced additional capital rules, bank capital levels increases, create a Capital Conservation Buffer, and required banks to have additional capital beyond required levels to mitigate ineffective capital practices.

## Chapter 8: Training

This chapter discusses the importance of training employees and stakeholders at all levels within banks. The need for training has been highlighted after the continuous passing of new compliance laws and the severity of risk exposure stemming from lack of knowledge.

## Part 3: Compliance Environment and Effective Leadership Practices

This part of the book discusses BSA AML practices when implemented within a framework that includes executive management at the governance and board levels. The use of effective leadership can garner success in the banking sector when top leadership acts as a champion of code of ethics.

## Chapter 9: Sanctions

This chapter discusses banks actions to ensure they do not violate the various levels of sanctions imposed by international governments. The United States sanctions are imposed against countries, companies, and individuals that banks are prohibited from conducting business.

## Chapter 10: Office of Foreign Assets Control (OFAC) Compliance Practices

Office of Foreign Assets Control (OFAC) implements and manages US economic sanctions. This chapter looks OFAC maintains a website which entails countries, companies, and individuals who act on behalf of terrorist that are placed on a blocked person list known as a Specially Designated Nationals (SDN) and Blocked Persons List. Countries that are on a blocked list are prohibited from sending funds to and from these nations.

## Chapter 11: Capital Requirements – Effective Practices

This chapter discusses effective compliance requirements such as maintenance of effective and independent compliance consistent with the organizational objectives; clear definition of data source for compliance analytics; ensure compliance monitoring and reporting activities promptly to upper management; top leadership must be a champion of code of ethics; strong morals and integrity; right products for clients; understanding regulatory compliance.

## Chapter 12: BSA AML Compliance Practices – Effective Practices

This chapter discusses BSA AML practices when implemented within a framework that includes executive management at the governance and board levels can garner success in the banking sector. An in-depth review of various lines of defenses involved in the monitoring of the compliance environment in the bank which includes: (i) First line of defense are business level executives/managing directors (create policies and procedures, personnel communication); (ii) Second line of defense Chief Risk Officer (monitoring of AML/CFT policies) independent of business line responsibilities; (iii) Third line of defense – internal audit (audit banks activities and report to audit committee) working collectively to create a low-risk control environment.

Part 1

# Regulatory Compliance in Domestic and Global Banks

# Chapter 1

# Regulatory Compliance Requirement and Practices

Many large global banks in the United States and around the world have complained about the increase in regulatory compliance laws that have placed stress both financially and operationally on their business practices. Hogan (2021) mentioned new regulations subsequent to the Dodd–Frank Act of 2010 increased banks' average total noninterest expenses by USD 50 billion per year and caused them to reduce or discontinue many products and services such as residential mortgage lending. Many of these compliance laws became more stringent after the 2008 recession relating to capital inadequacy, increase in money laundering, terrorist funding, sanctions, mortgage lending, and redlining laws. The increased risk of bank runs caused by significant banks going out of business due to significant losses, not enough capital to absorb these idiosyncratic losses and continue business, at risk banks not making payments on their debt obligations to other banks, has contributed to a collapse in the banking sector. The US and global banking regulators have enforced regulatory compliance laws to minimize bank risks (money laundering, terrorist funding, human trafficking, fraudulent banking activities, bad mortgage loans) that exposed them to significant losses which banks have complained that it is over regulation. In the United States, the regulatory compliance laws heavily impact Bank Holding Companies (BHCs), International Holding Companies (IHCs), commercial banks struggling to meet regulatory compliance requirements that requires reporting (daily, monthly, quarterly, annual) to various government regulators who oversees these compliance laws. Money laundering, fraud, and capital inadequacy have caused strain on banks from being monitored by numerous regulators in the United States, such as the Office of the Comptroller of the Currency (OCC), the Federal Reserve System (Fed), the Federal Deposit Insurance Corporation (FDIC), and the Office of Thrift Supervision (OTS) (Hogan, 2021). Since the banking sector is interconnected globally, the US government agencies have worked with international banking government agencies to combine their efforts in mitigating global bank risks.

US law enforcement agencies works with task forces, domestic and international, to coordinate their efforts with the Financial Crimes Enforcement Network (FinCEN) and financial institutions (FIs) to fight money laundering

**Compliance and Financial Crime Risk in Banks, 3–13**

Copyright © 2024 Sophia Beckett Velez

**Published under exclusive licence by Emerald Publishing Limited**

**doi:10.1108/978-1-83549-041-920241001**

(Johnson & Desmond Lim, 2002). Financial Action Task Force (FATF) established in 1989 by G7 countries (United States, Japan, Germany, France, United Kingdom, Italy, Canada) to prevent global money laundering expanded its focus to include counter terrorism after the September 11, 2001, terrorist attack and financial crimes (Meral, 2020). FATF established the international anti-money laundering (AML) standards, counterterrorist financing measures, and expanded to include 32 members (Australia, Austria, Belgium, Brazil, China, Denmark, Finland, France, Germany, Greece, Ireland, Netherlands, Spain, Sweden, Switzerland, Italy, Iceland, Japan, Canada, Luxembourg, Mexico, Norway, Portugal, Russia, Singapore, Turkey, New Zealand, the European Commission, the Gulf Cooperation Council (Meral, 2020). FATF performs periodic audits, evaluation of the global member countries systems to prevent money laundering, terrorism finance, and published in October 2016 Correspondent Banking Services document which reflected severe penalties for banks related to AML (Meral, 2020). Bank examiners received significant feedback and comments in 2017 relating to the burdens compliance requirements place on the business operations as it relates to Bank Secrecy Act/Anti-Money Laundering (BSA/AML), capital, call reports, Community Reinvestment Act (CRA) (DeMenno, 2020). Fed and other government agencies tackling the prevention of money laundering through BSA/AML laws require banks to implement an effective AML program which they continue to evaluate.

The AML program should cover the BSA laws and control activities (prevent, detect, monitor) designed to mitigate the breach of these laws. The BSA laws in the United States govern the citizens' transactions and require banks to disclose information about their customers to the federal government (Gladstein, 2021). The application of AML laws takes an all-inclusive effort where everyone is a stakeholder in the process of fighting this gruesome act. The fight against AML will require the official regulations of the financial system to include all parties involved such as banks, FIs, securities dealers, and all businesses including money services (Meral, 2020). On the global fronts, General Assembly of the United Nations at the Vienna Convention in 1988 tried to stomp out money laundering with the efforts of the G7 group of nations through the establishment of FATF that examines measures to fight money laundering and the sale of illegal drugs (Johnson & Desmond Lim, 2002). In 1990, the FATF issued 40 recommendations, comprehensive strategy action items against money laundering (Johnson & Desmond Lim, 2002). The global growth of fraud and money laundering spread through the global economy and was linked to 2%–5% of the global gross domestic product (Andrew, 2021). Global money laundering was aligned to illicit funds produced through grand corruption, laundering carried out through complex layering schemes that pass the funds off as legitimate, concealing illegal funds making them hard to detect and their origins (Andrew, 2021). Money laundering schemes range from $800 billion to $2 trillion illegal funds filtrated into the safe haven of western FIs using layering and washing schemes that are used to pass them off as legitimate transactions, causing economic instability (Andrew, 2021). Meral (2020) mentioned there are significant amount of illegal funds from criminal activities and terrorism which affects all countries' security and economic stability. Money laundering transfers illegal criminal money through laundering activities that conceal sources(drugs, smuggling, gambling, racket, kidnapping, robbery, trafficking women and children) and pass them into the legal financial system (Meral, 2020). Many of these illegal activities thrive in an environment with laxed or weak control activities. The weak internal control and AML programs were seen as a root cause of these FIs' failure to prevent these money laundering schemes. These illegal activities are sometimes tied to terrorism funding activities which the United States is actively trying to prevent and monitor.

The United States have levied sanctions against many of the terrorism-related nations/countries and created a list of countries US institutions and citizens are prevented from doing business. These US-imposed sanctions on countries were extended to include companies and individuals that banks are prohibited from conducting business transactions. US sanctions violations are treated as liability offenses and individuals can be found guilty/liable for committing a civil violation of sanctions without their knowledge of the act or degree of fault (Eckert, 2021). In 2012, sanctions violations civil penalty up to $65,000 per violation were levied on organizations assisting people to travel to Cuba, a nation on the sanctions list (Sullivan, 2018). There is the 2014 plea deal BNP Paribas made in relation to sanctions violation, agreeing to $8.9 billion fine and legal actions against 45 employees (Rose, 2020). The knowledge of the significant fines and penalty attached to being found in violation of sanctions has jolted the degree of seriousness banks have taken these violations. This has bolstered the serious nature of the preventative controls and business decisions taken to avoid this risk of sanctions violation. This is evident where several banks have turned to de-risking their portfolio of clients they conduct business activities because of enhanced due diligence; additionally, there are significant cost incurred to monitor activities that could be in violation of AML and counterterrorist financing regulation (Rose, 2020). There are strategic locations such as doing business near South America, Cuba, and Middle East that carries a higher exposure risk of being found in violation of sanctions or terrorist funding laws due to the high risk of crime associated with these areas and their client base. Banks have seen this de-risking strategy as a preventative measure that will reduce costs associated with monitoring and onboarding, lowering sanctions and reputation risks (Rose, 2020). Many banks feared that human error or failure of detecting an act of money laundering or fraud was not a viable excuse of being found in breach of sanctions and AML laws. This was evident where many banks face significant penalties related to transactions with individuals or entities related to a sanction's regime (Eckert, 2021). Banks were fined when their controls were ineffective over the end location and use of funds, even on situations where there is no actual breach of sanctions (Eckert, 2021). The idiosyncratic growth of money laundering forced global government agents to react with more stringent requirement for banks to implement preventive, detective, monitoring, and timely reporting of monitoring results of global banks AML program.

Banks are required to implement AML control activities to prevent and deter financial and cybercrimes. As part of AML laws, bank managers are required to complete a Suspicious Activity Report (SAR) that is used to track suspicious activities and identify customers those are involved with money laundering, fraud, and terrorist funding (Rifai & Tisnanta, 2022). Banks are expected to implement various teams that addressed cybersecurity, fraud prevention units, BSA/AML management boards, AML intelligence units, AML analysts/investigators, risk departments, and trained network administrators (Rifai & Tisnanta, 2022). Customer due diligence activities initially carried out at the onboarding of a new customer is an ongoing process throughout the business relationship with the bank; the transaction history of the customer should be reviewed looking particularly at the nature of the actual pattern of transactions against the pattern initially communicated by the customer (ElYacoubi, 2020). Senior bank managers should be actively involved in analyzing the results of customer transaction frequency assessments particularly high-risk customers, Politically Exposed Person (PEPs), and examination of triggered alerts (ElYacoubi, 2020). BSA laws in the United States established a $10,000 daily cash reporting threshold (Gladstein, 2021) which banks use in their daily surveillance and AML programs. Several international foreign governments have established similar threshold for monitoring and reporting of the AML-related transactions as well. Ecuador's Superintendency of Banks issued regulations that established the reporting of currency transactions over $10,000 or its equivalent in foreign currency (Johnson & Desmond Lim, 2002). Venezuela government efforts to fight anti-drug, AML, and unrestrained gambling houses industry enforced the Superintendency of Banking laws requiring the reporting of all transactions $10,000 or 4.5 million bolivars or more, reporting of suspicious transactions, and requiring banks to set up internal financial investigation units (Johnson & Desmond Lim, 2002). Banks have quarterly and annual reporting requirements of their effectiveness with these AML monitoring exercise established by the government and regulators. The failure of banks to block money laundering and fraudulent activities is often met by incurring penalties and fines.

Banks that fail to detect and prevent money laundering schemes and activities received significant fines from local domestic government agents and foreign government bodies. AML and compliance regulations have caused banks to become worried about the ramifications of them being found in noncompliance with these rules. Demetis and Angell (2006) posit that banks could receive heavy fines and jail sentences if bank employees inadvertently allowed a money launderer to operate on their watch. Meral (2020) noted institutions that are found to be in noncompliance with AML legal requirements receive punishments and possible sanctions. For example, several FIs had to pay large fines as they did not implement appropriate preemptive measures to prevent AML, and charges increased from $26.6 million dollars as of 2011 to $3.5 billion as of 2012 (Meral, 2020). The Hong Kong and Shanghai Banking Corporation (HSBC) is a global bank headquartered in London with subsidiaries in the United States; HSBC USA failed to implement properly designed AML program monitoring of suspicious account in areas such as Mexico and the program was poorly staffed (Rathod, 2022). The failure of the banks' AML monitoring program to prevent illegal acts in heavily exposed areas in South America has exposed them to the receipt of penalties from the Fed and other government regulators. The weakness and ineffectiveness of HSBC AML compliance programs have made them vulnerable domestically and internationally to money laundering illegal acts occurring on their watch without detective and preventive measures stopping the occurrence of these transactions. HSBC USA monitoring program failed to prevent physical purchase of billions of US dollars, bank notes from affiliates (Rathod, 2022). This was evident where HSBC received penalties in the United States and overseas. Regulators emphasize the serious nature of banks that are deemed noncompliance with the AML laws by levying penalties on banks and confiscating assets of perpetrators who take part in AML acts. There are penalties and findings levied on banks who fail to implement timely effective compliance programs and meet the reporting guidelines established in these compliance laws. HSBC was found in violation of the BSA laws, the International Emergency Economic Powers Act (IEEPA) and Trading with Enemy Act (TWEA) (Rathod, 2022). The court documents revealed that HSBC and its subsidiaries allowed the processing of illegal transactions across banned countries like Cuba, Iran, and Libya and permitted transaction to narcotic traffickers and money launderers (Rathod, 2022). HSBC banks' AML compliance programs were ineffective and inadequate on foreign correspondent account holder, which were some of the root causes within the failure of the AML system to prevent fraud (Rathod, 2022). HSBC agreed to its employee criminal conducts and the deferred prosecution agreement by department of justice (DOJ), forfeited $1.256 billion, and paid $665 million civil penalties (Rathod, 2022). The funds from the penalties were allocated to the various government regulators where OCC received $500 million out of $665 million civil penalties and the Office of Federal Reserve received $165 million (Rathod, 2022). On the global front, HSBC faced separate actions by Financial Service Authority (FSA), UK (Rathod, 2022).

The FSA authority levied penalty on Abbey National in the amount of £2.3 million for inadequate AML procedure and inadequate practice by failing to report suspicious banking transactions in a timely manner to the National Criminal Intelligence Service (NCIS) government agency (Webb, 2004). Abbey National took over a month to report 58% of suspicious transactions to NCIS; the institution failed to carry out proper due diligence identity checks on new customers by securing and examining appropriate documents (Webb, 2004). As a result of the lack of effective onboarding due diligence, 32% of new accounts were opened without the appropriate documentation; many of these weakness at Abbey National delayed reporting per regulatory requirements, resulted in lack of awareness about AML customer identification requirements in opening new accounts (Webb, 2004). Onboarding due diligence is seen as key to banks' Risk-Based Approach (RBA). RBA should be a part of the initial customer onboarding process with consideration given to the applicable four identified risk areas(geographic risk, customer risk, product risk, delivery channels) where potential risk posed by the customer is examined (ElYacoubi, 2020). Banks should identify the high-risk types of customer accounts at the onset of onboarding (trusts, PEPs, omnibus accounts, Power of Attorney [POA] accounts, private banking, pooled accounts); many of these accounts belong to gatekeepers (accountants, lawyers, professionals) which lacks transparency of the identity of the underlying clients/business owner and is not disclosed to the FI (ElYacoubi, 2020). There is over reliance on know your customer (KYC) and AML information relating to these gatekeeper and customer due diligence risk posed by delivery channels due to lack of face-to-face interactions (ElYacoubi, 2020). Prior to onboarding the customer, banks need to have an understanding of what purpose will the account be used for and the nature of the transactions. This will help them in making an assessment of the risk profile of this particular customer (high, medium, low) and make a determination if they want to conduct business with this type of customer. ElYacoubi (2020) posed several questions (is the customer intention to mainly perform online transactions? avail from private banking investments? is there an intention to establish offshore trust account with private bank? will this be simply a basic bank account?) where the answers to these questions will help gather pertinent information to assess customer risk prior to onboarding. Bank should address compliance risks assessment from the beginning and establish the purpose/nature of the banking relationship (ElYacoubi, 2020). High-risk customers at a minimum should be monitored and reassessed annually, medium risk every two years, and low risk every three years. ElYacoubi (2020) mentioned high-risk customers' reputation should be assessed by bank to gain an understanding of the type of institutions and jurisdictions they have business relationships with and consider if they have AML/CFT controls in place. The KYC/CDD laws require banks to establish customer identity, nature of transactions, validate funding, and assess customers' AML/CFT risks through KYC's customer process (ElYacoubi, 2020). The failure to do so results in penalties and findings on the banks.

Additionally, penalties are levied on criminals through the AML laws, but this has failed to deter or lower the numerous criminal acts by these offenders (Rifai & Tisnanta, 2022). Government prosecutors bypass the judicial process to confiscate illegal proceeds and asset used in these AML schemes. Criminals' punishment for money laundering acts is incarceration which is ineffective and insufficient in deterring money laundering acts (Rifai & Tisnanta, 2022). The global government has utilized asset recovery methods to take control of criminal assets used in money laundering fraudulent schemes without having to levy a penalty on the perpetrator referred to as Non-Conviction Based (NCB) Asset Forfeiture (Rifai & Tisnanta, 2022). The NCB Asset Forfeiture methods use assets suspected of being the proceeds of criminal actions portrayed as legal subjects, with countries represented by money laundering investigators' prosecutors against assets suspected of criminal acts proceeds and confiscate them without judicial judgment (Rifai & Tisnanta, 2022). Another area of focus for international banks compliance programs lies in prevention of mortgage fraud which was heavily underscored during the periods leading up to the 2008 recession and thereafter.

Banks' compliance programs have become more intensified after 2007 mortgage scandal to address prior regulations DeMenno (2020) referred to as mortgage lending requirements (Truth-in-Lending Act [TILA] of 1968, the Flood Disaster Protection Act of 1973, the Real Estate Settlement Procedures Act of 1973, the Home Mortgage Disclosure Act [HMDA] of 1975, CRA of 1977) and enhanced these laws. New regulations introduced during and after the Dodd–

Frank Act of 2010 increased banks' noninterest expenses an average of USD 50 billion per year and caused banks to discontinue or reduce their participation in several products and services including residential mortgage lending (Hogan, 2021). Prior to the passage of the Dodd-Frank Act of 2010, there was excessive risk-taking, mortgage fraud, predatory lending, managerial slack, risk shifting, and the issuance of bad loans by originators and arranges due to a weak risk management that played a role in causing the 2008 recession (Lui, 2011). Many banks lend to less credit-worthy customers that incurred a lot of losses and were less securitized (Chockalingam et al., 2018). These toxic mortgages were one of the main contributors to the 2008 crisis and were linked to residential mortgage-backed securities (MBSs) provided by one of the largest US lenders in subprime mortgages, Countrywide Financial Corporation (Coffee, 2018). This meltdown of the subprime mortgage sector was felt on the domestic and global fronts. In Japan, banks incurred losses on subprime mortgage-related products book value ¥54 billion March 2008 a revaluation loss of ¥1 billion and a realized loss of ¥46 billion (Tsung-Ming, 2017). Citigroup suffered losses in the third quarter between $8 billion and $10 billion stemming from a write-down in its direct holdings of $43 billion of collateralized debt obligations (CDOs) relating to subprime mortgages (Bartlett, 2012). National Australia Bank in 2001 suffered $2.2 billion loss due to product issues and model errors in their home mortgage subsidiary (Ganegoda & Evans, 2013). Another area in the mortgage that is high risk and generates significant losses is commercial real estate (CRE) loans. CRE loans are the second-largest loan types after the subprime mortgages the federal regulators act as an invisible hand in facilitating the continuance of these high risk in banks and the global financial sector (Croasdale & Stretcher, 2011). These CRE loans are issued by banks for the construction of new homes and development projects that tend to go into default due to nonpayments of these loans based on the lack of income/cash flow coming in while projects are construction in progress (Croasdale & Stretcher, 2011). Deutsche Bank AG incurred $300 billion in CRE losses for its share of the $3.4 trillion in outstanding CRE debt (Croasdale & Stretcher, 2011). The Fed intervenes on numerous occasions guaranteeing the loans and encouraging these banks to restructure the loans instead of taking foreclosure proceedings (Croasdale & Stretcher, 2011). The significant investments in subprime mortgage, other high-risk mortgages products despite the risky nature of these investments and process, have been incentivized by government programs and regulators.

These risky investments in the bad loans were incentivize by the Fed CRA which provides incentives for banks to take more risk or go broke from negative spreads (Allison, 2017). The CRA was used as a tool by the Fed to place pressure on banks to expand subprime lending through government-sponsored enterprises Freddie Mac and Fannie Mae failures (Allison, 2017). Hogan (2021) mentioned MBSs and CDOs were tools used by banks to take on risky investments that bypass the risk-based capital (RBC) ratios requirements set to ensure banks had sufficient capital. The low-risk weights assigned to MBS and credit default swap (CDS) in the design of the risk weighting system incentivized banks to increase their asset holdings in these highly risky products that were underrated by regulators (Hogan,

2021). MBSs issued or guaranteed by US government agencies received a moderate risk weight of 0.2 which was viewed by bankers to be advantageous and diversified their investment basket with a significant holding of these products (Hogan, 2021). One of the advantageous features of MBS was the regulatory capital cost was extremely low comparative to their rates of return (Hogan, 2021). To provide buyers with easy access to these types of risky products being passed to the public as low risk, the assets were structured as diversified baskets of loans securitized that allow buyers access to so-called diversified tranches with varying degrees of risk (Hogan, 2021). This so-called low-risk diversified tranches of MBS offered to public came crashing down during the great recession. These misguided ratings given to MBS were also assigned to CDOs that many in the finance markets considered to be a ratings mismatch which was demonstrated in the 2008 financial crisis where regulators severely underestimated the CDOs and MBSs riskiness (Hogan, 2021). This blunder by regulators played a major role in the systemic spread of risk related to CDOs and MBS throughout the financial system leading up to the collapse and 2008 recession (Hogan, 2021).

Banks were penalized if they did not cooperate where regulators wouldn't approve mergers unless the banks are actively conducting subprime lending; these misguided loans of Freddie Mac and Fannie Mae amassed liabilities of $5 trillion, including $2 trillion of subprime mortgages failures (Allison, 2017). The housing boom and aggressive lending activity increased bank risk and caused significant losses leading to a financial crisis (Egly et al., 2016). BHCs were heavily engaged in first and second home mortgage lending that have a high default rate (Dandapani et al., 2017). In 2012, JPMorgan Chase & Co. was faced with legal proceedings regarding its malpractice and activities in the origination and servicing of mortgages and paid a total settlement of USD 5.3 billion and USD 1.9 billion relating to the allegations of irregularities in its mortgage foreclosure activities (Strebel et al., 2016). In addition, JPMorgan Chase & Co. paid USD 13 billion in penalties relating to misrepresentation to the public and to investors of the sale of several MBSs in 2013 (Strebel et al., 2016). The use of fictitious and inaccuracies in loan appraisal reports were some of the underlining contributors to the mortgage scandal contributing to the recession.

The inaccuracies in real estate appraisals were noted as deeply flawed areas in the mortgage underwriting process that contributed to the mortgage scandals during the great recession. Many of the appraisal reports were intentionally incorrect to mislead the parties involved in the loan process. DeMenno (2020) states the inflated real estate appraisals identified as a part of the root cause of mortgage crisis were linked to lenders that put pressure on the appraisers. This was highlighted in 2007 petition filed by appraiser with over 11,000 signatures to Federal Financial Institutions Examinations Council (FFIEC) stating that lenders placed pressure on them to inflate real assets estimated value (DeMenno, 2020). The complaints highlighted bank directors' attention being displaced as they are forced take on voluminous compliance and management task that divert their attentions from the regular running of the business (DeMenno, 2020). The appraisers filed comments placed partial blame on weak corporate governance, lack of appropriate board oversight that contributed to regulatory failures prior and post crisis (DeMenno, 2020). The complaint filed by appraisers highlighted the role of appraisals in preventing real estate asset bubbles, the CRA of 1977 community development corporations and projects, and regulations pursuant to CRA geographic areas (DeMenno, 2020).

The lack of sufficient capital to cover significant losses in bank during the 2008 recession led to Basel III and Dodd–Frank Wall Street Reform and Consumer Protection Act (DFA) enacted in the United States in July 2010. There is compliance guidance issued for banks to use to develop effective strategies and policies to meet capital adequacy requirements of Basel III (Boora & Kavita, 2018). It is mandatory for banks to meet the Basel III Capital requirements by maintaining the larger proportion of bank capital as high quality and be able to demonstrate this in their Comprehensive Capital Analysis and Review (CCAR) stress test (Wall, 2017). These enhanced capital regulations requirement is reinforced through Dodd–Frank Wall Street Reform and Consumer Protection Act (DFA) enacted in the United States in July 2010 to contain systemic risk and foster financial stability (Allen et al., 2016). The Fed imposed CCAR and Dodd–Frank Act stress testing (DFAST) testing of minimum capital ratios for banks to ensure they are meeting the minimum capital to mitigate the risk of insolvency should they be exposed to significant losses; they would have enough capital to absorb the losses and to prove to regulators in the event of a potential financial crisis damage does not snowball and spread throughout the wider economy leading to bank runs (Lee, 2015). Fahey (2016) mentioned banks are required to demonstrate that their balance sheet fare well in a hypothetically adverse and severely adverse scenario required by the Fed; the assumption provided by the Fed for bank to use includes stock market crashes, significantly high unemployment used in preparing the CCAR submissions of up to 10,000 pages (Fahey, 2016). Boora and Kavita (2018) identified several factors that need to be in place to make Basel III risk management efforts effective such as: nation needs additional funds, capable humans, resources for proper implementation of these norms, strong capital base of banks.

In a prior study conducted by Sophia Velez, PhD, to identify effective capital regulation practices, compliance practices were examined. A qualitative e-Delphi study was used to build consensus among 10 banking finance experts across the United States on how to recognize a senior manager's effective practice toward capital regulation in large banks. The use of purposive sampling was employed to solicit participants to form a panel with experience in the underlining study constructs. The participants were recruited via social media (LinkedIn groups). The initial survey had five questions with subsequent follow-up rounds. The individuals were elected as part of a panel of expert participants because of their background in banking and knowledge on the subject. The inclusion criteria for selecting the panel of experts for the e-Delphi study is as follows: (1) adult over the age of 18; (2) employed a minimum of 10 years in the banking industry; (3) possession of an MBA in Finance; and (4) currently employed as a consultant to a large bank in the United States. The conceptual framework for the study employs Compliance and Ethics Group's (OCEG) principal–agent theory and goal theory as lens to examine the extant literature and the survey statement/responses (Velez, 2020). OCEG combines governance, risk management, internal control, assurance, and compliance through measurable tools that may enhance effectiveness and efficiency practices (Bezzina et al., 2014). There was one overarching research question (Velez, 2020) as follows:

- What is the level of consensus among banking finance experts across the United States on how to recognize a senior manager's effective practice toward capital regulation in BHCs?

There were five questions based on the OCEG concepts Velez (2020) which were used to design the questionnaire. The questionnaire asked experts to list at least six important factors relating to the following Round 1 questions:

- What governance practices can senior bank managers implement toward capital regulation that can be effective in reducing losses in BHCs?
- Describe risk management practices senior bank managers implement toward capital regulation that can be effective in reducing losses in BHCs.
- Describe internal control activities senior bank managers can implement toward capital regulation that can be effective in reducing losses in BHCs.
- How can assurance practices be implemented by senior bank managers toward capital regulation that can be effective in reducing losses in BHCs?
- Describe compliance practices senior bank managers can implement toward capital regulation that can be effective in reducing losses in BHCs.

The experts were asked to rate each statement on the second-round questionnaire against two separate (desirability and feasibility) 5-point Likert scales. Desirability measure ranged from (1) highly undesirable to (5) highly desirable, and feasibility ranged from (1) definitely infeasible to (5) definitely feasible (Linstone & Turoff, 1975). The instructions asked panelists to explain their reasoning for the allotted rating:

- (1) – Highly undesirable: Will have major negative effect.
- (2) – Undesirable: Will have a negative effect with little or no positive effect.
- (3) – Neither desirable nor undesirable: Will have equal positive and negative effects.
- (4) – Desirable: Will have a positive effect with minimum negative effects.
- (5) – Highly desirable: Will have a positive effect and little or no negative effect.

Each item on the feasibility scale:

- (1) – Definitely infeasible: Cannot be implemented (unworkable).
- (2) – Probably infeasible: Some indication this cannot be implemented.
- (3) – May or may not be feasible: Contradictory evidence this can be implemented.
- (4) – Probably feasible: Some indication this can be implemented.
- (5) – Definitely feasible: Can be implemented.

The Round 1 results relating to compliance practices toward capital regulation effective in loss reduction generated 23 statements. The panel of expert's recommendations for compliance in the first-round questionnaire of 23 statements were used in the second round of the questionnaire aligned to the following subcategories: compliance, reporting, technology, ethics, training, liquidity risk, partnership. The panelists made references collectively to the Round 1 questionnaire risk identification, communication, and responsibilities as effective practices that can be used to recognize a senior manager's effective practice toward capital regulation in BHCs. Round 2 generated 15 items, and Round 3 had 6 items that met consensus. The consensus level was set to six or more out of the ten votes. The panel of experts' voting results on maintenance of effective and independent compliance consistent with the organizational objectives, clear definition of data source for compliance analytics, compliance monitoring and reporting activities promptly to upper management, top leadership must be a champion of code of ethics, understanding regulatory compliance reflected varying degrees of desirability and feasibility which corroborates the extant literature.

# Chapter 2

# Regulatory Compliance in Global Banks

Global banks with complex structure that entails multiple entities (swap dealer, broker dealer, commercial banking, bank holding company, investment banking, real estate business vehicle) are faced with compliance regulations from many different regulators (Federal Reserve Banks, Financial Industry Regulatory Authority (FINRA), National Association of Securities Dealers (NASD), Commodity Futures Trading Commission (CFTC), Securities Exchange Commission (SEC), Federal Deposit Insurance Corporation [FDIC], Financial Action Task Force [FATF]) all at once or simultaneously. Compliance regulations in the United States encompass Bank Secrecy Act/anti-money laundering (BSA/AML) requirements which include currency transaction reporting (CTR) thresholds, suspicious activity reporting (SAR), response to 9/11 Know Your Customer (KYC) requirements, the frequency and thresholds for reporting have intensified (DeMenno, 2020). AML entails a combination of actionable items (policies, laws, regulations) working together to stomp out financial crimes; AML covers cybersecurity that aims to prevent cybercrimes through implementation of legislation requirements (Rifai & Tisnanta, 2022). There is the Corporate Transparency Act (CTA) effected by Treasury Department who establish a beneficial ownership registry to assist the agency in unveiling and chasing bad actors (Bieler, 2022). Financial Crime Enforcement Network (FinCEN) published cybersecurity guidelines that regulate financial services and combined cyber incidents with AML programs (Rifai & Tisnanta, 2022). A requirement is to incorporate compliance units in every Information Management and Information Security departments and make them active stakeholders (Rifai & Tisnanta, 2022). Banks have been historically required to gather KYC information about a customer to fulfill the compliance regulatory requirements and build a profile that is used to designate suitable products and services (ElYacoubi, 2020). However, banks have been slowly moving toward a futuristic approach where the customer information is viewed as merely big data (ElYacoubi, 2020). The human connection of interacting and knowing your customer has been shifted to knowing the data and the analytics versus trends; a more quantitative approach is taken instead of the personalized qualitative approach. As such, bank relationships will not be providing the required customer information, and there is a shift in the financial

Compliance and Financial Crime Risk in Banks, 15–25
Copyright © 2024 Sophia Beckett Velez
Published under exclusive licence by Emerald Publishing Limited
doi:10.1108/978-1-83549-041-920241002

system from KYC era to know your data (KYD) era (ElYacoubi, 2020). This KYD era is slightly delayed in the United States with heightened levels of money laundering activities due to its location and proximity to high-risk money laundering nations in South America. Money laundering has evolved over the years from the historical drug trade to other activities (profits of numerous other offenses/organized crime, white-collar crimes/corruption, prostitution, arms trading, tax fraud) which all have negative economic impact on countries and reputational damage to bank branches (Teichmann & Marie-Christin Falker, 2021). The Society for Worldwide Interbank Financial Telecommunications (SWIFT) system is aiding US government in cracking down on some of these cross-border money laundering activities and terrorist funding.

The SWIFT system was designed with KYC Registry which provides information about the customers in international trade across borders, which mitigates the money laundering risk through the sharing of information to respective authorities (Meral, 2020). This cross-border sharing of information using this application takes place with maximum transparency and will aide authorities to combat US$ 500 billion to US$ 1 trillion criminal income laundered via banks annually, half of this amount flows through American banks (Meral, 2020). However, the SWIFT-related operational controls have its challenges linked to decentralized SWIFT operations encompassing several SWIFT nodes at branches which are subject to being compromised (Ghosh, 2021). Branches with high number of users with access to the SWIFT system exposed banks to higher degree of risk of user credentials being compromised leading to high levels of fraud (Ghosh, 2021). This high-risk exposure of user access to SWIFT is partially linked to a lack of adequate oversight controls over the SWIFT operations and the delegation of appropriate individuals as SWIFT administration; instead, junior officers are wheeled with financial power beyond the delegated officer, paired with over reliance on vendors on varying matters related to SWIFT (Ghosh, 2021).

On the global fronts, UK banks are plagued with financial crime increase; Russia has 400 banks and 47 exchange bureaus run by criminal groups which the FATF are helping the Russians to prevent money laundering; Mexico (bank drafts, peso exchange market, electronic transfers) used these out bound currency smuggling techniques to launder dirty money (Meral, 2020). This illegal income from activities of organized crime committed by the mafia has negatively impacted the political and economic structure of social and corporate life (Meral, 2020). The UK compliance regulations stipulate SAR reporting conditions in their AML framework under the Proceeds of Crime Act (POCA) 2002, which sanctions individuals for failure to report suspicious transactions to the respective regulator (Loh, 2021). There are POCA 2002 sections (330,331) that deal with the failure to file SAR; section 330 addresses bank employee having direct handling of client transactions, while 331 applies to bank money laundering reporting officer responsible for handling the disclosures made by bank employees (Loh, 2021). The failure to file SAR penalties were applicable to banks and other financial institutions.

The penalties and punishment issued to banks and other financial institutions for being not in compliance with SAR requirements as noted in AML laws have been astronomical. There were significant charges (MoneyGram International $100 million, First Bank of Delaware $15 million) for violation of money laundering laws in 2012, TD Bank NA $37.5 million in 2013, JP Morgan Chase Bank $461 million in 2014 for violations/deficiencies of AML compliance programs (Meral, 2020). There are other financial institutions that had charges (Courts & Company £8.75 million between 2007 and 2010, ING bank paid $619 million for US sanctions violations 2012, London based HSBC pay over $1.5 billion penalty again for Swiss private banking assisting customers in tax evasion (Meral, 2020)). The Hongkong and Shanghai Banking Corporation (HSBC), London, paid French authorities $370 million dollars for tax evasion, $100 million payment to American Justice Department for currency transactions charges, and $1.92 billion punishment for money laundering in the United States (Meral, 2020). There has been a low conviction hurdle establish for the lack of filing a SAR; as such, bankers have taken precautionary measures by filing large number of reports on a just in case basis to avoid criminal liability (Loh, 2021). The United Kingdom filed 36% of the total number of SARs filed in EU countries between 2006 and 2014 which contributed to an uptick of 10% in number of SARs file with the National Crime Agency (NCA) (Loh, 2021). Banks are required to perform KYC procedures as part of the Customer Due Diligence (CDD) utilizing principles articulated in four key elements of KYC (customer acceptance policy, customer identification procedures, monitoring of transactions, risk management) policies (Ghosh, 2021). Similarly, ElYacoubi (2020) highlights the importance of CDD in ensuring financial institutions know their customers who they are, the nature of the transaction, who they are holding funds for, and the identify of any potential risk the bank is exposed to from entering these transactions. CDD documents the individuals identifying, validate this information (customer's name, address, date of birth, official identification) based on the documents received (ElYacoubi, 2020). In addition to CDD, banks have to keep records safe and provide training to employees (Loh, 2021). AML and compliance regulations have caused banks' fears to grow that they could receive heavy fines and even jail sentences if bank employees inadvertently allowed a money launderer to operate; to minimize the risk of occurrence banks moved from face-to-face KYC checks to an automated process (Demetri's & Angell, 2006). The automated process has a vulnerability to its operation due to the lack of human interaction and rationale applied in live scenarios when interacting with customers.

The removal of the manual interaction with customers reduced critical thinking, on the spot assessment and review by management. The system and programming logic used to automate the process generated a significant number of false positives (Demetri's & Angell, 2006). This left compliance agents scrambling to review a great deal of transactions to be identified as Suspicious Transaction Reports (STRs); updates made to legislative requirement enlarge the scope of money laundering, thereby impacting increase in volume of STRs (Demetri's & Angell, 2006). The increase in volumes does pose a detection risk where a true positive threat might be overlooked/not spot due to overwhelming amount of data. Banks try to compensate or mitigate some of the risk by layering more technology in that area. This layering of more technology approach is evident in the bank's compliance and AML departments where technology is heavily used to analyze and identify potential issues. The use of layers of technology to address the new regulatory demands posed new challenges for banks as these multiple systems do not speak to each other. Instead, they operate in silos and data do not flow from one system to another. This poses the challenge of managing huge volumes of data in multiple legacy and new systems. Data management became an additional risk the bank must face. Velez (2020) mentioned statements centered on data management principles failed to meet the 60% consensus threshold. Velez (2020) argued the failure of data management statements to pass to Round 3 supports arguments made by Alampalli (2013) that when regulatory data are on separate information systems, this pose a challenge of accessibility to the teams who use these data and preempts the routine sharing of information. The financial system and regulatory compliance have changed significantly, but the regulatory tools and data collection methods were not aligned to address new requirements (Alampalli, 2013). The information system frustration banks face with the demand for information and systems capabilities is reflective in the panel's unfavorable ratings of statements around data infrastructure (Velez, 2020). These statements Round 2 votes are displayed below Tables 2.1 and 2.2 (Velez, 2020).

Table 2.1. Compliance Data Source Practices 2nd Round Data: Nonconsensus.

| Statement | Ratings | Total Number of Panelist Who Selected Each Ratings |
|---|---|---|
| Statement 65 – Compliance practices toward capital regulation that can be effective in reducing losses include clear definition of data source for compliance analytics. | | |
| | Highly undesirable: Will have major negative effect. | 0 |
| | Undesirable: Will have a negative effect with little or no positive effect. | 1 |
| | Neither desirable nor undesirable: Will have equal positive and negative effects. | 1 |
| | Desirable: Will have a positive effect with minimum negative effects. | 0 |

Table 2.1. *(Continued)*

| Statement | Ratings | Total Number of Panelist Who Selected Each Ratings |
|---|---|---|
| | Highly desirable: Will have a positive effect and little or no negative effect. | 4 |
| | Definitely infeasible: Cannot be implemented (unworkable). | 0 |
| | Probably infeasible: Some indication this cannot be implemented. | 0 |
| | May or may not be feasible: Contradictory evidence this can be implemented. | 0 |
| | Probably feasible: Some indication this can be implemented. | 4 |
| | Definitely feasible: Can be implemented. | 5 |

AML regulations strive to facilitate transparency as pointed out by Gerbrands et al. (2022) through the use of KYC responsibilities, reduce secrecy, and report suspicious transactions. This information helps law enforcement agencies to detect and prosecute money laundering actors (Gerbrands et al., 2022). Money laundering facilitates illegal income/cash from fraudulent sources (black money, dirty money, illicit money earned from illegal transactions) to enter the financial system by concealing the source of the income (Mearl, 2020). Money laundering is a tool/strategy drug dealers funnel (dirty money, black money, illicit money) from illegal sources and pass them as legal activities; the launderer/criminal conceals the illegal crime income from the authorities with the intent to use it within the economic system (Meral, 2020). Criminals have used money laundering tactics to disguise illegal origin of criminal proceeds by recycling its surplus of criminal money and injecting it into the legal economy (Gerbrands et al., 2022). Revenues from criminal activities (drugs, human trafficking, cybercrime, fraud) are laundered through multiple channels in banks in different ways (Gerbrands et al., 2022). Ghosh (2021) mentioned FATF and Basel Committee on Banking Supervision (BCBS) launched AML standards, while banking regulators globally

Table 2.2. Compliance Reporting Practices 2nd Round Data: Nonconsensus.

| Statement | Ratings | Total Number of Panelist Who Selected Each Ratings |
|---|---|---|
| Statement 66 – Compliance practices toward capital regulation that can be effective in reducing losses include monitoring and reporting activities promptly to upper management. | | |
| | Highly undesirable: Will have major negative effect. | 0 |
| | Undesirable: Will have a negative effect with little or no positive effect. | 0 |
| | Neither desirable nor undesirable: Will have equal positive and negative effects. | 2 |
| | Desirable: Will have a positive effect with minimum negative effects. | 1 |
| | Highly desirable: Will have a positive effect and little or no negative effect. | 3 |
| | Definitely infeasible: Cannot be implemented (unworkable). | 0 |
| | Probably infeasible: Some indication this cannot be implemented. | 1 |
| | May or may not be feasible: Contradictory evidence this can be implemented. | 0 |

Table 2.2. *(Continued)*

| Statement | Ratings | Total Number of Panelist Who Selected Each Ratings |
|---|---|---|
| | Probably feasible: Some indication this can be implemented. | 5 |
| | Definitely feasible: Can be implemented. | 3 |

worked on strengthening AML measures within the banking system the engagement of three lines of defense in effective risk management. These lines of defense are imperative in mitigating AML and countering terrorist funding (CFT) which includes: (i) First line of defense (concise policies and procedures, personnel communication), (ii) Second line of defense (monitoring of AML/CFT policies by chief officer independent of business line responsibilities), (iii) Third line of defense – internal audit that independently conducts AML/CFT audit (Ghosh, 2021). Banks are required to perform the necessary due diligence to legitimize the identity of customers and prove the validity of their business transactions. Ghosh (2021) stated banks should pursue business relations with potential customers after they have performed the due diligence per FATF recommendations, and only then should they establish banking relationship after the identity of customer has been satisfactorily established and verified. Banks are required to file STR as per regulatory requirements when they are not satisfied with the true identity of customer (Ghosh, 2021).The panel of experts' votings in the second round on AML/KYC requirements reflected very low desirability. Some initial second round voting on AML/KYC statements desirability and feasibility ratings from the panel of experts are noted below. These statements Round 2 votes are displayed below Tables 2.3 and 2.4 (Velez, 2020).

Banks find that there is a significant increase in the volumes of activities they file with FinCEN with little outcomes and action taken to slow the rate of criminal activity. Gladstein (2021) noted leaks from FinCEN in 2020 revealed Western banks took part in the significant flow of billion dollars dirty and corrupt money, which were diverted to the coffers of the Davos elite with virtually none of the money launderers going to prison. Only a few executives from Iceland, Ireland, and Spain regions and four bankers in the world were sentenced to jail time for contributing to the global financial crisis (Gladstein, 2021). Gerbrands et al. (2022) stated individuals set up companies and slip the criminal turnovers into global and local company's cash register. In some scenarios, cash couriers are used and complex international constructions of shell companies, with established bank accounts in different countries (Gerbrands et al., 2022). These shell

Table 2.3. Compliance Policy Practices 2nd Round Data: Nonconsensus.

| Statement | Ratings | Total Number of Panelist Who Selected Each Ratings |
|---|---|---|
| Statement 59 – Compliance practices toward capital regulation that can be effective in reducing losses include establishing and communicating compliance policy across pertinent organizations. | | |
| | Highly undesirable: Will have major negative effect. | 0 |
| | Undesirable: Will have a negative effect with little or no positive effect. | 0 |
| | Neither desirable nor undesirable: Will have equal positive and negative effects. | 1 |
| | Desirable: Will have a positive effect with minimum negative effects. | 4 |
| | Highly desirable: Will have a positive effect and little or no negative effect. | 3 |
| | Definitely infeasible: Cannot be implemented (unworkable). | 0 |
| | Probably infeasible: Some indication this cannot be implemented. | 0 |
| | May or may not be feasible: Contradictory evidence this can be implemented. | 0 |

Table 2.3. *(Continued)*

| Statement | Ratings | Total Number of Panelist Who Selected Each Ratings |
|---|---|---|
| | Probably feasible: Some indication this can be implemented. | 3 |
| | Definitely feasible: Can be implemented. | 6 |

Table 2.4. Compliance Risk Identification Practices 2nd Round Data: Nonconsensus.

| Statement | Ratings | Total Number of Panelist Who Selected Each Ratings |
|---|---|---|
| Statement 60 – Compliance practices toward capital regulation that can be effective in reducing losses include identification of compliance risks and controls at the relevant organizational level. | | |
| | Highly undesirable: Will have major negative effect. | 1 |
| | Undesirable: Will have a negative effect with little or no positive effect. | 1 |
| | Neither desirable nor undesirable: Will have equal positive and negative effects. | 2 |
| | Desirable: Will have a positive effect with minimum negative effects. | 1 |

*(Continued)*

Table 2.4. *(Continued)*

| Statement | Ratings | Total Number of Panelist Who Selected Each Ratings |
|---|---|---|
| | Highly desirable: Will have a positive effect and little or no negative effect. | 3 |
| | Definitely infeasible: Cannot be implemented (unworkable). | 0 |
| | Probably infeasible: Some indication this cannot be implemented. | 0 |
| | May or may not be feasible: Contradictory evidence this can be implemented. | 3 |
| | Probably feasible: Some indication this can be implemented. | 1 |
| | Definitely feasible: Can be implemented. | 5 |

companies receive and lend money with counterfeit bills and make mortgage payments to each other bypassing real economic activity (Gerbrands et al., 2022). This fraudulent international circulation of money passes through complex corporate constructions on average five times around the world before being used for (real estate, business, expensive cars, jewelry) purchases. This level of sophisticated fraudulent disguise of money laundering activity has caused regulator to heighten stricter AML laws. Gerbrands et al. (2022) mentioned AML policies became stricter as time progressed, updates made to KYC rules, wide range of financial and nonfinancial institutions (second-hand car dealers, real estate agents) have been included as required agents/business places are required to report suspicious transactions which is a new deterrence to criminals.

Banks made several complaints and comments regarding BSA of 1970. DeMenno (2020) mentioned there were over 125 comments regarding AML regulations issues. Many of the AML issues noted relate to complaints filed about CTR thresholds, processes for SAR, and KYC requirements (DeMenno, 2020). There are complaints from small community banks that these compliance regulations do have some impacts on their day-to-day routines. DeMenno (2020) noted small community banks were impacted by compliance rules, and there should be consideration given to a tiered regulatory approach. This tiered regulation would reduce regulatory burden on small and community banks which has been a central component of recent financial reform legislation (DeMenno, 2020). Small community banks provided lending comments that addressed mortgage lending requirements for the following regulations: Truth-in-Lending Act (TILA) of 1968, the Flood Disaster Protection Act of 1973, the Real Estate Settlement Procedures Act of 1973, the Home Mortgage Disclosure Act (HMDA) of 1975, and the Community Reinvestment Act (CRA) of 1977 (DeMenno, 2020). These overlapping regulations have placed a regulatory cost strain on monthly, quarterly, and annual reporting and monitoring of these laws. DeMenno (2020) asserted banks and a few public interest groups commented on the three-day 'right of recession' requirement in relation to Regulation Z and Truth-in-Lending Act of 1968. The complains were met with positive outcomes, more action-oriented, updated frequent clarifying materials issued and revision of some of seven of the rules as well as the revision of at least seven rules (DeMenno, 2020). These revisions were issued in 2017 and were related to rule that addressed capital, regulatory reporting, real estate appraisals, safety, and soundness examination frequency, and BSA (DeMenno, 2020); Sarbanes-Oxley Act 2002 (SOX) received several complains at first launch as it was seen as over regulation on firms who were required to be compliant with Section 404(b) of the Act reporting on company's internal controls (Coffee, 2018). The absorbent costs small companies incurred to become SOX compliant caused them to push back on the regulation and was quickly cut back by both legislative and regulatory action (Coffee, 2018). Similarly, Dodd–Frank Act set the level at $50 billion to be classified as a systematically important financial institution (SIFI) and received significant complaints and push backs which caused the regulators to increase the level to $250 billion to be classified as SIFI which was too high (Coffee, 2018). There were other changes/updates to policies and rules that addressed community banks complaints relating to the issuance of clarifying for appraisal waiver processes, evaluations as alternatives to appraisals, food insurance guidance, development of a community bank call report, appraisal threshold levels were raised for commercial real estate loans (DeMenno, 2020).

# Chapter 3

# Compliance Requirements in Bank Holding Company and International Holding Companies (IHC)

Compliance costs have increased for banks, and regulators have seen an increase in their monitoring costs of compliance (Hogan, 2021). Banks in the United States are regulated by several agencies (Office of the Comptroller of the Currency [OCC], Fed, Federal Deposit Insurance Corporation [FDIC], and the Office of Thrift Supervision [OTS]), of which the OCC was the first to propose risk-based capital (RBC) rules in the late 1980s (Hogan, 2021). The RBC rules were for national banks and then the Fed for bank holding companies (BHCs) which overtime these agencies jurisdiction overlaps (Hogan, 2021). The compliance budgets for the Fed, FDIC, and OCC/OTS from 2001 to 2017 doubled, largest increase came in 2010 with the passage of the Dodd–Frank Act 2010 and after Dodd–Frank rules were finalized, which increased regulations 2012 and 2013 (Hogan, 2021). Regulators costs doubled and banks' compliance costs significantly increased (Hogan, 2021). Regulators such as the OCC and OTS have an increase in their compliance regulations monitoring cost of USD 7 million and USD 6.2 million to their agencies, along with increased compliance costs of USD 74 million for national banks and USD 136.7 million for savings associations (Hogan, 2021). Some of the significant increases in banks compliance costs are related to complex tracking and reporting systems to meet the enhanced compliance requirements, hiring of additional head count to meet man hours demands posed by these regulations, and cost relating to loss of business due to these requirements. The Fed requires banks to perform stress test, which is a complex act, and report the results to regulators within an established timeframe. Stress test requires a significant amount of human and monetary resources, use of several quantitative models to produce the calculations required, which is constrained/hampered by internal organizational silos, outdated software systems, and internal bureaucracy (Denev & Mutnikas, 2016). Stress test requirements articulated in capital regulation posed a challenge for banks to meet as laid out by the Feds. Capital regulation laws (Dodd–Frank Act 2010, Basel III) do not

Compliance and Financial Crime Risk in Banks, 27–35
Copyright © 2024 Sophia Beckett Velez
Published under exclusive licence by Emerald Publishing Limited
doi:10.1108/978-1-83549-041-920241003

identify acceptable ways to conduct the stress tests of capital, which is still a work in progress (Kapinos & Mitnik, 2016). The use of models to perform stress as suggested by the federal regulators has been ineffective, which prompted bankers to decapitalize their banks and pass the cost of their risk-taking to taxpayers (Dowd & Hutchinson, 2016). The Fed performs independent stress test of banks, which found their capital did not meet requirements articulated in the capital regulation laws; Fed required Bank of America in 2015 to raise new capital and caused the bank to spend $100 million to develop its 2015 resubmission; Citigroup spent $180 million in preparation for its 2014 submission (Walker et al., 2017). Banks have incurred astronomical cost to perform stress test and to meet capital restrictions imposed by the Fed.

Many large US banks feel the restrictions placed on business activities by these enhanced regulatory compliance requirements by the Fed have made them less competitive; these capital compliance demands were placed by the Fed without any regard to banks maintaining profitability or international competitiveness, which posed a threat and burden to banks competitiveness (Fahey, 2016). Compliance activities such as stress tests is a complex onerous activity, which many bank executives complained pulled them away from mission-critical business objectives (Lee, 2015). Bank executives find themselves thrust into months of data compilation, and potentially tense meetings with regulators (Lee, 2015). Many bank directors made several complaints that their focus on strategic business initiatives has been diverted to numerous regulatory compliance requirements and management functions burden (DeMenno, 2020). Despite the complaints from banks, Congress is commissioned to act as a mitigation effort to prevent another event such as the 2008 recession from remerging without measures in place to address the impacts. Congress implemented a multiagency regulatory approach to financial regulation using multiple overlapping agencies; Commodity Futures Trading Commission (CFTC) relied on Chicago Mercantile Exchange and National Futures Association (NFA) to monitor derivative transactions in banks that contributed to the 2007–2008 financial crisis (Fischer, 2015). These new and enhanced regulations are to pre-empt events that led to 2008 recession from reoccurrence such as bankruptcy of major investment banks Bear Stearns and Lehman Brothers from losses they incurred from subprime mortgage (Deos et al., 2015). These losses triggered Central Banks in the United States and around the world to launch bailouts to rescue impacted banks from the domino effects from these losses and prevent insolvency of too-big-to-fail (TBTF) banks (Deos et al., 2015). The US Troubled Asset Relief Program (TARP) authorized by Congress in October 2008 authorized USD 700 billion bailout funds of which USD 313 billion was disbursed to banking/financial sector (Velez, 2020). Germany and UK central banks bailed out their TBTF financial institutions where the European Central Bank financial statements grew by 241% (Hale, 2016; Dodd–Frank Act 2010 aim to mitigate some of these risks posed by TBTF banks). This heightened compliance regulations in US banks have to do with banks TBTF stature which imposed Dodd–Frank Act of 2010 Capital Adequacy rules on them and other problems stemming from the US proximity to South America, which plays a role in banks acting as agents in money laundering fraudulent events.

The TBTF stature of US Banks because of their size and global reach posed a systemic risk to the global banking industry and economy. These banks are classified as significant financial institutions (SIFI) multinationals whose significant losses have negative impact on the global banking and financial sector. A part of the Fed mitigation strategy is to have banks maintain Tier 1 capital of 4% of average consolidated on-balance-sheet assets, a supplementary leverage ratio calibrated against a bank's on-balance-sheet assets and off-balance-sheet exposures (Herring, 2016). Tier 1 capital ratio requires banks to choose between increasing their lending margins and reducing their risk-weighted assets and be mindful that they are required to hold high quality liquid assets (Paulet, 2016). The low capital balances banks kept prior to the great recession has forced the Fed to require banks to keep a minimum net capital, perform quarterly and annual stress testing of their capital, and report the results quarterly and annually to the assigned federal regulators. Dodd–Frank Bill 2010, Section 165 require banks: (1) maintains a minimum capital amount that is convertible to equity in times of financial stress, (2) enhanced public disclosures, (3) short-term debt limits, including off-balance-sheet exposures, (4) a catchall provision allowing prudential standards and the Board of Governors involvement (Wan, 2016). The minimum net capital ratio of 8% is required by BHC (Tanda, 2015). The Fed regulatory powers were strengthened to govern respective areas of Section 165(b), where Section 165(b)(1)(A) lists mandatory standards: (1) risk-based capital requirements and a leverage limit of no greater than 15:1, (2) liquidity requirements, (3) risk committee with risk management requirements, (4) a resolution plan incase needed, (5) credit exposure report, (6) concentration limits (Wan, 2016). In Section 165(b)7, the Fed gain prudential powers to conduct stress testing of minimum capital using models (Wan, 2016). Fed requires BHC to conduct two kinds of annual stress tests: A Comprehensive Capital Analysis and Review (CCAR) and Dodd–Frank Asset Stress Tests (DFAST) to demonstrate their meeting the capital ratio requirements (Herring, 2016). The results are filed with the Fed annually. Baradaran (2014) noted that the bank's use capital plan actionable items help to determine if the CCAR requirements stipulated by the regulators if stressful conditions emerged they would still meet the minimum capital ratios expectations. Basel II enforced the need for capital adequacy phased in to meet the deadlines by 2015 (Sanders, 2015). Central banks supervise the ability of the banks to withstand stress and ensure the banking system becomes and remain sound (Dowd, 2015). Basel III, as noted by Hogan (2021), revised the risk weights of the Advanced Approaches system and market risk rule to exclude credit rating–based risk assessment as per Dodd–Frank Act Section 939A. Through Basel III, there were increase in capital rules and capital levels, adding of Capital Conservation Buffer requirements, and additional level of capital when banks are paying dividends to shareholders and executive (Hogan, 2021). Additionally, new rules were implemented by the regulators relating to Liquidity Coverage Ratio (LCR) and Net Stable Funding Ratio (NSFR) required minimum levels of high-quality liquid asset (HQLA) holdings as percentages of expected cash outflows (Hogan, 2021). The regulators established the guidelines for the HQLA weights based on each asset's perceived level of liquidity; these levels are required for banks to be maintained in addition to bank capital rules requirements (Hogan, 2021). The regulators emphasized to banks that they must demonstrate they will remain in compliance for five specified minimum capital ratios at the end of a nine-quarter, severely adverse stress scenario (Herring, 2016). The Fed conducted their own independent stress test of capital scenarios of the banks results were disappointing, implying deterioration of banks' capital positions and several large banks needed a significant capital injection to keep their capital levels above the minimum requirement levels (Kapinos & Mitnik, 2016). One of the backlash banks received from the regulators for lack of maintaining the minimum capital requirement is a restriction of freedom to make dividend distributions and employee bonus payments (Davies, 2015). This was evident in the case of Deutsche Bank and Santander US when they failed the stress tests and capital requirements imposed by the Fed; they were prohibited from paying dividends and stock buybacks (Walker et al., 2017).

Regulatory compliance measures emphasized in the Dodd–Frank Bill 2010, Section 165 as a result of the 2008 recession were met with resistance from bank management. The financial regulatory system has been described as complex, bureaucratically specialized, interconnected, and it can facilitate the risk of fragmentation and duplication (DeMenno, 2020). Many bank managers stated that providing financial information quarterly and annually to several different regulators is a burden and overregulation. They feel the different regulators are asking for different forms of the same business transactions; there are instances where Fed, OCC, Securities Exchange Commission (SEC), and Finra are within the same year collecting audit evidence from the same bank which they do not leverage among themselves or share. Alampalli (2013) mentions financial regulators are faced with difficulty of sharing data because the submitted data are stored on separate information systems that is inaccessible to the various teams; this prevents the routine sharing of information between the regulators. This inefficiency has caused banks to reproduce the same data for different regulators which takes their time and attention from the day to day running of the business to meet shareholder requirements. Many complained the strenuous nature of the compliance requirement shift their focus from normal running of the business to meeting the reporting guidelines of Dodd–Frank Bill 2010. Some initial second round voting on compliance statements that had low desirability and feasibility ratings from the panel of experts are noted below. These statements Round 2 votes are displayed below in Tables 3.1–3.4 (Velez, 2020).

The use of assessment and test prior to implementation of a regulation and monitoring of the performance of the regulation after implementation has been touted by management as a measure to justify the need of that regulation. Business management in general believes that there should be some sort of regulatory test/regulatory impact assessment (RIA) completed by regulators to justify the implementation of capital requirements and liquidity rules imposed on banks, which was examined between 1986 and 2018 (Hogan, 2021). An examination of cost–benefit analysis (CBA)/RIA of 27 proposed RBC and liquidity rules issued between 1986 and 2018, nine of these rules had RIA, five noted this will create net benefits, while two cited sources indicate the rule's net benefits will be negative rather than positive (Hogan, 2021). Banks have mixed feelings that new or increased regulations will have positive impact on their business. CBA is

Table 3.1. Compliance Practices on Forward Looking Science 2nd Round Data: Nonconsensus.

| Statement | Ratings | Total Number of Panelist Who Selected Each Ratings |
|---|---|---|
| Statement 10 – Compliance practices toward capital regulation that can be effective in reducing losses includes forward looking science. | Highly undesirable: Will have major negative effect. | 2 |
| | Undesirable: Will have a negative effect with little or no positive effect. | 2 |
| | Desirable: Will have a positive effect with minimum negative effects. | 2 |
| | Highly desirable: Will have a positive effect and little or no negative effect. | 2 |
| | Definitely infeasible: Cannot be implemented (unworkable). | 2 |
| | Probably infeasible: Some indication this cannot be implemented. | 2 |
| | May or may not be feasible: Contradictory evidence this can be implemented. | 1 |
| | Probably feasible: Some indication this can be implemented. | 2 |
| | Definitely feasible: Can be implemented. | 3 |

Table 3.2. Compliance Practices on Long-Term Strategies 2nd Round Data: Nonconsensus.

| Statement | Ratings | Total Number of Panelist Who Selected Each Ratings |
|---|---|---|
| Statement 11 – Compliance practices toward capital regulation that can be effective in reducing losses includes actively promote long-term strategies to ensure deficiencies do not recur. | Highly undesirable: Will have major negative effect. | 1 |
| | Undesirable: Will have a negative effect with little or no positive effect. | 0 |
| | Neither desirable nor undesirable: Will have equal positive and negative effects. | 2 |
| | Desirable: Will have a positive effect with minimum negative effects. | 2 |
| | Highly desirable: Will have a positive effect and little or no negative effect. | 2 |
| | Definitely infeasible: Cannot be implemented (unworkable). | 1 |
| | Probably infeasible: Some indication this cannot be implemented. | 1 |
| | May or may not be feasible: Contradictory evidence this can be implemented. | 2 |
| | Probably feasible: Some indication this can be implemented. | 4 |
| | Definitely feasible: Can be implemented. | 3 |

Table 3.3. Compliance Practices Tests 2nd Round Data: Nonconsensus.

| Statement | Ratings | Total Number of Panelist Who Selected Each Ratings |
|---|---|---|
| Statement 16 – Compliance practices toward capital regulation that can reduce losses includes tests that measure compliance with regulatory requirements. | Highly undesirable: Will have major negative effect. | 1 |
| | Undesirable: Will have a negative effect with little or no positive effect. | 1 |
| | Neither desirable nor undesirable: Will have equal positive and negative effects. | 0 |
| | Desirable: Will have a positive effect with minimum negative effects. | 2 |
| | Highly desirable: Will have a positive effect and little or no negative effect. | 3 |
| | Definitely infeasible: Cannot be implemented (unworkable). | 0 |
| | Probably infeasible: Some indication this cannot be implemented. | 0 |
| | May or may not be feasible: Contradictory evidence this can be implemented. | 1 |
| | Probably feasible: Some indication this can be implemented. | 4 |
| | Definitely feasible: Can be implemented. | 6 |

Table 3.4. Compliance Practices Periodic Assessment 2nd Round Data: Nonconsensus.

| Statement | Ratings | Total Number of Panelist Who Selected Each Ratings |
|---|---|---|
| Statement 62 – Compliance practices toward capital regulation that can be effective in reducing losses includes periodic assessment of compliance adherence with metrics. | Highly undesirable: Will have major negative effect. | 0 |
| | Undesirable: Will have a negative effect with little or no positive effect. | 1 |
| | Neither desirable nor undesirable: Will have equal positive and negative effects. | 1 |
| | Desirable: Will have a positive effect with minimum negative effects. | 2 |
| | Highly desirable: Will have a positive effect and little or no negative effect. | 2 |
| | Definitely infeasible: Cannot be implemented (unworkable). | 0 |
| | Probably infeasible: Some indication this cannot be implemented. | 0 |
| | May or may not be feasible: Contradictory evidence this can be implemented. | 0 |
| | Probably feasible: Some indication this can be implemented. | 1 |
| | Definitely feasible: Can be implemented. | 7 |

used to analyze economic policies to identify net benefits for society and highlight those that might cause negative impacts; those policies that are beneficial to society are encouraged to undertake and ones deemed harmful are discouraged from implementation (Hogan, 2021). There are banks who have a firm belief that Dodd–Frank Act placed excessive burden on banks, comparative to credit unions and Fintech companies who have very few new requirements (DeMenno, 2020). There are concerns about large banks remaining competitive and how do the stack against nonbank institutions such as shadow banks (DeMenno, 2020). Shadow banks tend to compete with regular bank for business while not being required to be Dodd–Frank compliant. Capital regulation incentivized regulatory arbitrage; huge migration of traditional banking deals was transferred to shadow banking activities (Lin et al., 2018). This was used as a tool to diversify bank asset portfolio by undertaking shadow banking that produced superior return performance in a high-risk environment (Lin et al., 2018). The lack of commitment to prudential rules and supervision is problematic; this incentivized traditional bank to explore the use of shadows banks and contributed to a significant amount of risk in the banking system (Crawford, 2017). Regulations that are poorly designed can unintentionally reduce financial stability by encouraging banks to increase their risk-taking activities and become costly to the business/banks (Hogan, 2021).

# Chapter 4

# Compliance Failures in Global Banks

Global banks have failed to implement an effective compliance program to address regulatory requirements of AML, Basel III, and Dodd–Frank 2012 Bill. The Hongkong and Shanghai Banking Corporation (HSBC) bank's anti-money laundering (AML) system failed to prevent fraud due to weakness in its compliance program (Rathod, 2022). HSBC failed to implement an effective AML program that monitors suspicious account among its HSBC group affiliates. HSBC USA had HSBC Mexico its largest customer regions, as required by the regulators which was demonstrated in the bank's activities 2006–2010 (Rathod, 2022). Rathod (2022) asserts risk screening for fraud can be achieved with the implementation of three lines of defense (bank operation unit risk owner as the first line of defense, risk review team as the second line of defense, chief AML compliance officer having complete control as the third line of defense). These three teams working closely together in a transparent manner with effective communication among them can improve the company's compliance program. The team will use enterprise-wide risk assessment (EWRA) program to identify, assess, and manage potential roadblocks to minimize financial crimes with the help of the AML compliance team (Duncan, 2021). The AML compliance team responsibilities include (report AML issues and recommendations, new AML trends dissemination, EWRA execution) assess money laundering risks (money laundering, terrorist financing, financial crimes) and the reporting of the outcomes to stakeholders (Duncan, 2021). The appropriate risk rating measures should be incorporated in the compliance framework to gain efficiencies which include risk identifications based on customer/business types and locations. The identification of risk based on customers (personal/business, local/foreign residents, low/medium/high-risk rating, business types, licensed and registered businesses, designated nonfinancial businesses, financial institutions), services (deposits, loans, wire transfers, credit, prepaid cards, ATM, e-commerce), countries (areas involving incoming and outgoing funds, locations of business operations, locations of account principals, areas that infiltrate the organization because of geographic proximity), and administration (number, structure, experience, authority of AML compliance employees, senior management, board involvement) are incorporated when assessing risk (Duncan, 2021). An effective

Compliance and Financial Crime Risk in Banks, 37–47
Copyright © 2024 Sophia Beckett Velez
Published under exclusive licence by Emerald Publishing Limited
doi:10.1108/978-1-83549-041-920241004

execution of EWRA entails enforcement of policies, record keeping, manual vs. automation in the monitoring system, computer-based systems, available reports, compliance officer, company-wide employee training, local laws compliance, regulations and guidance instructions, quality and timing of submitting Suspicious Transaction Report (STR) (response time to external requests), practices around sanctioned persons, frequent independent testing frequency, and correcting review findings/recurrence of issues (Duncan, 2021). This scrutiny should cover transactions capture face-to-face and remote (new account and operating), deposits, withdrawals by cash, international/local transfers, checks, ATM activities (Duncan, 2021). Risk rating measures identified in the EWRA and other fraudulent measures were ineffectively executed at HSBC Global bank.

During 2006–2009, HSBC assigned a low-risk rating to Mexico ignoring serious money laundering risk and opted to have lax AML control, which incentivized drug cartels and money launders to use the bank as their preferred financial institution (Rathod, 2022). HSBC, USA, failed to monitor and prevent HSBC, Mexico, $670 billion wire transfers and over $9.4 billion in purchases of physical US dollars deemed illegal and fraudulent (Rathod, 2022). Additionally, HSBC and its subsidiaries were penalized for failing to preempt the processing of illegal transactions throughout (Cuba, Iran, and Libya) and money laundering and narcotic traffickers' transactions (Rathod, 2022). As such, HSBC admitted it's employee criminal conducts and entered into an agreement with the department of justice (DOJ), forfeited $1.256 billion, and paid $665 million civil penalties (Rathod, 2022). The application of the risk rating (high, medium, and low) to a region, entity, and individuals is imperative in applying the correct set of controls to mitigate/prevent that risk event. European (Greek) sovereign debt received the lowest risk ratings despite their potential for default which incentivized German banks to enter into regulatory arbitrage and acquired large amounts of relatively high-yield sovereign debt (Hogan, 2021). This practice was replicated in the United States which exposed them to systemic risk where a single financial market caused the banking crisis that spread across continents (Hogan, 2021). This compliance system should have tough fraud risk control for know-your-customer (KYC), customer due diligence (CDD), and AML (Rathod, 2022). Similarly, Danske Bank was fined for failing to monitor suspicious transactions that were more than €200bn, a majority of which were linked to politically exposed persons (PEPs); this highlights the serious nature of the ramifications of money laundering and the scandals banks face when caught up in these scandals (Loh, 2021). Banks are punished by the regulators who have established measures in place to penalize banks when they fail to monitor and control their money laundering risk; these Money Laundering Regulations (MLRs) in 2017 levied expectations on banks to conduct CDD and retain the evidence and train their respective employees on these measures (Loh, 2021). Additionally, penalties (up to $500 a day, criminal fines up to $10,000, maximum of two years in prison) are issued by regulators to banks that failed to report beneficiary identification and other information required to them (Bieler, 2022).

CDD is a proposed preventive task bankers are required to execute to mitigate potential fraud and money laundering. Bankers are to assess potential clients posing a money laundering risk through assessment (verification, customer identification through reliable independent data, identification of beneficial ownership, business nature knowledge, suspicious transactions scrutiny) activities (Andrew, 2021). Individuals (real estate agents, lawyers, notaries, accountants, trust, and company service providers) that are non-financial professionals used as gatekeepers (Andrew, 2021). The UK and Canada legislation in relation to CDD requirements are more stringent where additional steps are used to identify individuals diagnosed as PEPs and apply enhanced measures as applicable (Andrew, 2021). The identification and tracking of beneficial owners have been a long sought after legislative action that would have unmasked their existence in anonymous corporate structures (Bieler, 2022). The Financial Action Task Force (FATF) regulatory body that sets AML standards first recommendations concerning beneficial ownership was in the 1990s, followed by groups (G7, United Nations, European Union) who implemented policies targeting beneficial ownership (Bieler, 2022). The ongoing surveillance of customer relationships and identification of beneficial owners are not required as part of the Customer Identification Program (CIP) in the United States (Andrew, 2021). However, the US Bank Secrecy Act (BSA), Patriot Act, and CDD rules have touched this goal including the Corporate Transparency Act (CTA) which the Treasury Department implemented a beneficial ownership registry to assist the agency in identifying and pursuing money launders (Bieler, 2022). This limitation in the CIP process posed a significant AML deficiency due to the lack of beneficial ownership details; this loophole fosters the creation of shell companies by trustees/registered under aliases (Andrew, 2021). Rathod (2022) mentioned inadequate CDD on foreign account holders coupled with an ineffective AML program can be the root cause of illegal transactions. Regulators targeted junior bankers to enforce personal criminal liability against them for failed CDD processes which would have been more impactful if brought against senior management (Loh, 2021). These personal liabilities brought against senior management would incentivize them to implement more effective CDD, record-keeping, employee training, and Suspicious Activity Report (SARs) filing processes (Loh, 2021). BSA rules were updated in 2016 to strengthen CDD requirements for new accounts opened at financial institutions for nonexcluded entities which required verification of beneficial owner identity (Bieler, 2022). The information needed is obtained on a standard certification form or substantive requirements laid out in the rule; financial institution can rely on the beneficial ownership information provided by the customer as long as there is no knowledge of facts that would make that information questionable which is then maintained in a database and provided to law enforcement upon request (Bieler, 2022). Financial Crime Enforcement Network (FinCEN) has deployed a Geographic Targeting Orders (GTO) program that uses the increased risk of high-end real estate to follow potential money launderers (Bieler, 2022).

Indonesia fights against AML as noted by Rifai and Tisnanta (2022) by incorporating cybercrimes legislations released by FinCEN to regulate financial services and cyber incidents within AML programs. One tool launched as part of the cybercrimes and AML program is the use of SAR to track suspicious activities and fulfill anti-money laundering laws; SAR identifies customers involved in money laundering, fraud, or terrorist funding (Rifai & Tisnanta, 2022). Ghosh (2021) mentioned that in countries such as India, banks are found to be noncompliance with regulatory requirements (fraud risk management, cyber security framework, Society for Worldwide Interbank Financial Telecommunications (SWIFT)-related operational control, anti-money laundering standards) which exposed them to compliance risk. This compliance failure related to banks not fully cognizant of the risk arising from compliance failures causing high economic costs, reputational risk, which resulted in fraud increased within the Indian banking sector (Ghosh, 2021). In 2014, Indian banks failed to meet regulatory compliance guidelines in relating to fraudulent losses to the tune of ' 8180 cr, frauds from lack of adequate due diligence with fixed deposits result in losses over ' 700 cr, bank officials fraudulent transactions resulted in the collapse of (Yes Bank, Lakshmi Vilas and Punjab, Maharashtra Co-operative) banks (Ghosh, 2021). There are instances of loan fraud at ICICI Bank involving bank officials in Trade-based Money Laundering (TBML) as a result of weakness in Indian banks (Ghosh, 2021). RBI imposed monetary penalties of ' 38.35 cr. on 26 public sector banks (PSB) and of ' 8.55 cr. on 8 private banks for noncompliance with regulations (Ghosh, 2021). Not only do banks have to worry about risks form money laundering, they face with risk from investment decisions and not meeting the compliance requirements around those investments.

Similarly, low risk rating incentivized banks to increase their investments in highly rated collateralized debt obligation (CDO) and mortgage-backed securities (MBSs) holdings because they deemed low risk by regulators (Hogan, 2021). Banks were incentivized to hold CDOs and MBSs rather than mortgage loans which was to their detriment as these assets produced significant losses greater than what was anticipated during the housing market collapse (Hogan, 2021). These risky MBS and CDO investments were partially blamed on the reliance on risk-based capital (RBC) ratios that were deemed unreliable in the assessment and prediction of risk levels. Hogan (2021) asserts RBC ratios are considered inferior predictors of risk, and they periodically encourage banks to increase their risk levels. This risk weighting system/methodology encouraged banks to increase investments in underrated risk products by the regulators and to strip investment assets whose risks are overrated. These incentives gave rise to schemes (mortgage fraud, predatory lending, managerial slack, risk shifting) that gave rise to the issuance of bad loans which thrived on a weak risk management environment (Lui, 2011). Banks in the United States increase their CDO and MBS holdings and resolved to a fire sale in 2008 after the prices began to fall which is a shared systemic risk exposure that spread losses and panic through the global banking system (Hogan, 2021). Europe rated sovereign debt at the lowest risk ratings despite default risk being high; German banks purchased large amounts of high-yield sovereign debt (Greek government debt) (Hogan, 2021). This incorrect risk rating exposed the global banking system to systemic exposure in a single financial market heightened in the panic phase of the European crisis link to the downgrade from A to BBB+ for Greek debt on April 21, 2010 (Hogan, 2021). Compliance risk identification and addressing issues statements Round 2 votes are displayed below Tables 4.1–4.3 (Velez, 2020).

Compliance programs experience blockages stemming from an increase in costs due to redundancy, environmental changes, and regulatory conditions (Helena & Madsen, 2021). There has been significant increase in technology cost

Table 4.1. Compliance Practices on Risk Identification 3rd Round Data: Nonconsensus.

| Statement | Ratings | Total Number of Panelist Who Selected Each Ratings |
|---|---|---|
| Statement 60 – Compliance practices toward capital regulation that can be effective in reducing losses include identification of compliance risks and controls at the relevant organizational level. | | |
| | Highly undesirable: Will have major negative effect. | 1 |
| | Undesirable: Will have a negative effect with little or no positive effect. | 1 |
| | Neither desirable nor undesirable: Will have equal positive and negative effects. | 2 |
| | Desirable: Will have a positive effect with minimum negative effects. | 1 |
| | Highly desirable: Will have a positive effect and little or no negative effect. | 3 |
| | Definitely infeasible: Cannot be implemented (unworkable). | 0 |
| | Probably infeasible: Some indication this cannot be implemented. | 0 |
| | May or may not be feasible: Contradictory evidence this can be implemented. | 3 |

*(Continued)*

Table 4.1. *(Continued)*

| Statement | Ratings | Total Number of Panelist Who Selected Each Ratings |
|---|---|---|
| | Probably feasible: Some indication this can be implemented. | 1 |
| | Definitely feasible: Can be implemented. | 5 |

Table 4.2. Compliance Practices on Responsibilities Clarity 2nd Round Data: Nonconsensus.

| Statement | Ratings | Total Number of Panelist Who Selected Each Ratings |
|---|---|---|
| Statement 61 – Compliance practices toward capital regulation that can be effective in reducing losses include ensure compliance function is adhered to with clarity of responsibilities and remediation steps for breaches are discovered. | | |
| | Highly undesirable: Will have major negative effect. | 1 |
| | Undesirable: Will have a negative effect with little or no positive effect. | 0 |
| | Neither desirable nor undesirable: Will have equal positive and negative effects. | 1 |
| | Desirable: Will have a positive effect with minimum negative effects. | 1 |

Table 4.2. *(Continued)*

| Statement | Ratings | Total Number of Panelist Who Selected Each Ratings |
|---|---|---|
| | Highly desirable: Will have a positive effect and little or no negative effect. | 3 |
| | Definitely infeasible: Cannot be implemented (unworkable). | 0 |
| | Probably infeasible: Some indication this cannot be implemented. | 0 |
| | May or may not be feasible: Contradictory evidence this can be implemented. | 2 |
| | Probably feasible: Some indication this can be implemented. | 2 |
| | Definitely feasible: Can be implemented. | 5 |

Table 4.3. Compliance Practices on Periodic Assessment 2nd Round Data: Nonconsensus.

| Statement | Ratings | Total Number of Panelist Who Selected Each Ratings |
|---|---|---|
| Statement 63 – Compliance practices toward capital regulation that can be effective in reducing losses include periodic assessment of issues and issues closures. | | |

*(Continued)*

Table 4.3. *(Continued)*

| Statement | Ratings | Total Number of Panelist Who Selected Each Ratings |
|---|---|---|
| | Highly undesirable: Will have major negative effect. | 0 |
| | Undesirable: Will have a negative effect with little or no positive effect. | 0 |
| | Neither desirable nor undesirable: Will have equal positive and negative effects. | 1 |
| | Desirable: Will have a positive effect with minimum negative effects. | 3 |
| | Highly desirable: Will have a positive effect and little or no negative effect. | 3 |
| | Definitely infeasible: Cannot be implemented (unworkable). | 0 |
| | Probably infeasible: Some indication this cannot be implemented. | 0 |
| | May or may not be feasible: Contradictory evidence this can be implemented. | 0 |
| | Probably feasible: Some indication this can be implemented. | 2 |

to meet the regulatory requirements. KYC requirements introduced by regulators as a response to 9/11 frequency and thresholds for reporting caused the significant generation of columns of data (DeMenno, 2020); banks turned to technology to aid in processing and reporting of KYC information. The KYC process was originally done face-to-face which later became automated, but logic of the system/technology design did not incorporate questions that were deemed awkward; questions phrased with the assumption technology was the solution and best method for KYC questioning (Demetri's & Angell, 2006). The result of this faulty design was KYC checks to an automated process (Demetri's & Angell, 2006). There was increased scrutiny placed on transaction and investigation, and doubtful entries are posted as a Suspicious Transaction Report (STR), which increased the volumes of STR and grew the number of reports. The generation of significant KYC volumes for review posed a detection risk problem true money laundering might be overlooked due to huge amount of data to be reviewed that posed a challenge. The KYC process is a continuous monitoring function as asserted by Ghosh (2021) that KYC should be periodically updated every two years, and banks may impose partial freezing of accounts. In situations where identity of customers becomes less satisfactory are required to file STR with the respective regulatory body (Ghosh, 2021).

Additional failures bank face is to prevent micro laundering funds washed and placed in bank accounts. Illegal transaction has emerged in other business vehicles through the use of online tools. Rifai and Tisnanta (2022) stated micro laundering is used by cyber criminals on websites (PayPal, job advertising sites, online and mobile micro-payments) that are connected with net banking services/or credit cards to prevent being detected by AML surveillances. As such, money launderers through this micro laundering work around able to move large sums of money through thousands of small electronic transactions which is difficult to detect (Rifai & Tisnanta, 2022). These criminals were undetected because of tools (virtual credit cards, prepaid e-sims in mobile phones, virtual currencies/Bitcoin, scammed bank account for instant transactions, PayPal account) that were used to process their money laundering activities (Rifai & Tisnanta, 2022). Cyber criminals hack money transfer mechanisms (wire transfers, online payments, cash deposits, withdrawals) through the use of fraudulent accounts opened with lost documents/documents of nominees hacked, fictitious companies that process these transactions in their accounts, and convert stolen funds into cash/cash withdrawals via ATMs (Rifai & Tisnanta, 2022). Another loophole Teichmann and Falker (2021) noted is so-called sterile investments in antiquities, jewelry, or other assets used to launder illegal funds. Money launderers have relocated their operations to sectors that are less regulations where large cash amounts can be deposited into illegal funds without attracting much attention (Teichmann & Falker, 2021). This goes undetected by the authorities because they are unable to trace origin and the money is then layered via techniques, cryptocurrencies, software program known as mixer that conducts several transactions in the darknet and pass through to the economy (Teichmann & Falker, 2021). The money can then be converted into fiat and integrated into the economy. Real estate is another money laundering tool that banks fail to detect and prevent money laundering; the purchase price is paid part in cash and cash for renovation using incriminated money for an undervalue property (Teichmann & Falker, 2021).

There are other failures linked to weak compliance program as per Helena and Madsen (2021) because of the challenges banks face in establishing an effective compliance program linked to the development of workplace silos. The existence of workplace silos is formed when individuals and groups within an organization work in a vacuum with little interaction/communication with other teams/groups (Helena & Madsen, 2021). This working in isolation with lack of cooperation/communication between different risk and controls teams leads to gaps in accountability and communication with other business units leading to redundancies and chaos (Helena & Madsen, 2021). The problems and risk at hand tend to grow larger and spread to other related and unrelated areas. The lack of communication with other departments when operating in silos/vacuum prevents these departments to implement preventative measures in place to prevent this issue from spreading to them and causing harm to their business operations. This is a challenge for the bank to implement the appropriate actionable activities to prevent the spread of the issue throughout their domestic and global operations. Duncan (2021) argued silos prevent management to see the entire picture of the flow of operations as no one department handles a transaction from beginning to end. It is hard to see the risk that lies in a process if you are unable to see the entire flow of the transaction. As such, risks associated with the activities flow in the same manner; this has influenced bank to decentralize AML functions, disassemble silos to clarity and transparency into the entire picture of a transaction, and add to enhance decision-making (Duncan, 2021). However, there are scenarios where decentralized tool might help banks move funds effectively among each other while deterring money laundering. Blockchain has been used by many SIFI banks in the United States and globally to fund their business transactions. Blockchain is a new technology tool that is decentralized used to move money; blockchain used set of interconnected units that speak to each other based on set rules of interaction (Kerimov et al., 2020). Blockchain stores data, combines storage decentralization, continuously duplicates registry of transactions while they remain anonymous; blockchain technology behaves as an open, decentralized, publicly distributed digital book; transactions between people are recorded on several computers making the record trail unable to change retroactively without changing all subsequent blocks of information and the network consensus (Kerimov et al., 2020). The use of blockchain among global banks has provided them with some level of comfort and trust when they transact among each other.

This technology uses cryptographic protocols and their combination to transfer digital information back and forth from sending node to receiving node within the network in large blocks (Kerimov et al., 2020). Each block is assigned a digital signature presented in a hash sum which is a unique identifier; the hash sum function dictates how the blocks are transferred in a particular order which cannot be changed generating a mismatch error between the structure and identifier in the system (Kerimov et al., 2020). There is no central administrator for blockchain, and there is a global distribution of equivalent copies in various countries; this new technology is used in the banking sector to improve the system of counteraction to criminal income legislations (Kerimov et al., 2020). Several financial services firms have invested in blockchains technology to minimize money laundering through build-in risk mitigation tools, customer identification, and transaction monitoring activities (Campbell-Verduyn, 2018). Blockchains have controls in place that create AML-compliant registries, identify holders of CC wallets in real-time manner, and create blacklists of users; countries such as Isle of Man built leading AML-compliant jurisdiction;

Singapore utilizes blockchain technologies with a national KYC platform (Campbell-Verduyn, 2018). Switzerland is working with various bodies, regulators, law enforcement, and financial service providers to identify the origin of Crypto Currency (CCs) (Campbell-Verduyn, 2018). While the implementation of the technological tools has been very helpful to many countries and businesses to aid in meeting their AML goals, cost to many businesses has been a burden, and many businesses have to shift their investment needs to make funding available for blockchain.

Part 2

# Compliance Laws and Requirements (BSA/AML)

# Chapter 5

# Implications of Compliance Weakness in Banks and Regulatory Penalties

The risk of not meeting government compliance requirement is referred to as compliance risk. Ghosh (2021) argues compliance risks are reflected in issues aligned to actions that are a result of noncompliance with (fraud risk management, cyber security framework, Society for Worldwide Interbank Financial Telecommunications (SWIFT) operational control, asset classification and provisioning, anti-money laundering [AML] standards sanctions rules) and regulatory capital requirements. In 2012, changes were made that impacted the capital requirements of banks through regulatory laws (Basel III) Office of the Comptroller of the Currency (OCC) revisions of risk weights of the Advanced Approaches system, updates made to market risk rule to exclude credit rating–based risk assessment required by Dodd–Frank Act Section 939A (Hogan, 2021). This was replaced with enhancements to capital rules by the OCC (increase capital levels, maintenance of a capital conservation buffer, additional level of capital required for banks to pay dividends and bonuses) which are required by US banks and savings associations (Hogan, 2021). Banks are required to perform quarterly and annual stress testing and report their results to the Federal Reserve Bank, Financial Industry Regulatory Authority (FINRA) requires the quarterly and annual Focus reporting, Securities Exchange Commission (SEC) requires annual Sarbanes-Oxley Act (SOX) certifications filing, and OCC requires annual filings. Banks who failed to prove they have met these costly and time-consuming compliance requirements are often penalized. Global banks found to be in noncompliance with regulatory compliance measures such as AML, Dodd–Frank Bill 2010, Section 165; Sanctions were dealt with harshly by the regulators. Fed requires banks to use models to perform stress testing on their capital which is one of the risk management efforts to address the risk posed by systemically important financial institutions (Allen et al., 2016). Capital stress test as a risk management effort has been a challenging tool to use effectively to address the systemic risk in the financial markets stemming from financial distress, systematically important financial institutions (SIFIs), and achieving financial stability (Allen et al., 2016). Banks are required to develop their own macroeconomic scenarios which entail

Compliance and Financial Crime Risk in Banks, 51–64
Copyright © 2024 Sophia Beckett Velez
Published under exclusive licence by Emerald Publishing Limited
doi:10.1108/978-1-83549-041-920241005

the use of a statistical model Vector Autoregression (VAR) that employs the dependency between macroeconomic drivers and modeling segments (Jacobs, 2016). The Fed performs their own independent capital projections computation under each scenario and compared them to the bank's capital projection, gaps/ shortfalls, and the Fed Capital Assistance Program (CAP); additionally, Fed had backstopped as a bridge to private capital for the capital shortfalls through CAP and stress tests (Gorton, 2015). Banks struggle to leverage the guidance provided by the Basel Committee as the volume of the proposed new regulations and supervisory practices were hundreds of pages; the system has become markedly more complicated (Herring, 2016). Stress tests use various scenarios in a multitude of quantitative models which experience roadblocks from internal organizational silos, bureaucracy, and legacy software systems which do not speak/transfer data easily from one system to another (Denev & Mutnikas, 2016).

There are difficulties in models being able to explore the relationship between capital adequacy and the boom-bust cycle in a financial crisis, financial conditions of intermediaries, and the business cycle, being able to analyze the relationships in the fluctuation of prices and entrepreneurs' debt (Fukuda, 2016). The human interaction and rationale used in data selection and input to the models is a weakness itself and subject to estimation errors. Many times, the raw data the banks used to feed the models are from underlying systems that are not connected/do not speak to each other, which impedes the completeness and accuracy levels for the data being used. Banks workarounds to lack of data flows and system interface by manually downloading and uploading data to the systems that will feed the models. This is subject to errors in the underlining data feeding these models used to project capital and loss levels. Bellof and Wehn (2018) noted models have statistical errors resulting from the selection of basic data period that is either shorter or longer calibration periods, different estimation procedures (stressed value-at-risk-figures, regular data), and the confidence intervals selected can produce estimation errors. This human involvement with the manipulation of the model posed a challenge to stress tests and could have contributed to lack of predictability of mortgage-backed risk (Allen et al., 2016). This can contribute to errors going undetected which is a limitation in stress testing by themselves being able to prevent another financial crisis (Allen et al., 2016). The lack of modes to predict failure in the financial market, capital requirements, significant losses and rapid decline in housing prices (Baradaran, 2014). As such, the accuracy of these stress test measures is being questioned and the possible danger to the banking sector and being unable to prevent destabilizing of that industry; this is aligned to the models lacking the capability to predict actual market risk and losses due to its heavy reliance on historical data and events and static balance sheet (Baradaran, 2014). Despite these concerns raised, banks are required to perform the stress test required by the regulators and prove they meet the minimal capital requirements; the lack of performing compliance requirements by the banks would subject them to fines/penalties and actions taken by the Fed.

Fed's stress test of selected banks' capital revealed their levels were inadequate which led to their concerns with the deterioration of banks' capital positions; Fed suggested several large banks will need a significant amount of capital injection to keep their capital levels and buffer above the minimum levels (Kapinos & Mitnik, 2016). For example, stress test of banks by the Fed in 2015 found Bank of America capital levels to be lower than required, and the bank was asked to raise additional capital and refile their capital plans; Bank of America spent $100 million to develop its 2015 resubmission; Citigroup spent $180 million for its 2014 submission; Morgan Stanley resubmitted a revised capital plan for 2016; Deutsche Bank and Santander US failed the stress tests and were prevented from paying dividends and conducting stock buybacks (Walker et al., 2017). Banks had to develop teams specifically dedicated to assist the stress testing process; they had to have model validation teams different from model risk managers (Goldberg, 2017). To improve the accuracy and completeness of the stress testing filings, banks' model risk management teams are required to develop and use sound models, governance, and control mechanisms; the bank leadership namely the board and senior management was required to oversee the stress testing/capital adequacy compliance requirements, with other controls measures implemented such as policies and procedures, controls and compliance, incentive, and organizational structure (Goldberg, 2017). To ensure employees had the skillset to meet the compliance requirements of Basel III, banks implemented training programs to upgrade the skills of their employees (Boora & Kavita, 2018). Banks needed to improve their technological infrastructure so that data quality and availability can achieve effective compliance (Boora & Kavita, 2018). Banks should use models to manage their compliance with the capital levels required and stress testing requirements; the lack thereof resulted in regulators imposes penalties on banks with far too little capital (Abou-El-Sood, 2017). Banks did not meet the required capital levels to be placed in receivership/conservatorship (Abou-El-Sood, 2017). The Fed actions against banks whose capital limits are not in compliance to prevent bank runs, as a measure to reinforce consumer confidence. The Fed believed the monitoring of capital and effectively responding with the tools available to them is effective; However, the Round 2 voting from the panel was low in response to this control activity. The panel Round 2 voting relating to Fed compliance requirements of capital limits/reactions, stress test, and use of models' statements Round 2 and Round 3 votes are displayed below Tables 5.1–5.7 (Velez, 2020).

On the AML fronts, Congress on January 1, 2021 made significant updates to AML Act that require banks to maintain beneficial ownership registry for selected entities (Bieler, 2022). This information for each beneficial owner/applicant (full legal name, date of birth, unique identifying number (passport number/driver's license number/Financial Crime Enforcement Network (FinCEN) identifying number, current residential/business street address) which should be made available if requested by the government from the bank (Bieler, 2022). A failure to report accurate and complete/updated information will result in a penalty up to $500 a day and may face criminal fines up to $10,000 or a maximum of two years in prison (Bieler, 2022). There is provision for individuals acting in good faith to correct the inaccurate information within 90 days of the submission; there are substantial penalties in place for unauthorized disclosure/use of the beneficial ownership information of $500 fine for each day of violation, charges up to $250,000, five years in jail, and additional severe penalties if there are other violations (Bieler, 2022). Banks such as the Hongkong and Shanghai Corporation (HSBC) because of the proximity of where they perform business activities have a greater exposure to fraud and being unable to mitigate AML breaches. Andrew

Table 5.1. Internal Control Practices on Timely Reporting 2nd Round Data: Nonconsensus.

| Statement | Ratings | Total Number of Panelist Who Selected Each Ratings |
|---|---|---|
| Statement 7 – Internal control activities toward capital regulation that can be effective in reducing losses include timely reporting of potential capital effects that will go a long way toward reducing losses in bank holding companies. | | |
| | Undesirable: Will have a negative effect with little or no positive effect. | 1 |
| | Desirable: Will have a positive effect with minimum negative effects. | 3 |
| | Highly desirable: Will have a positive effect and little or no negative effect. | 3 |
| | Definitely infeasible: Cannot be implemented (unworkable). | 1 |
| | Probably infeasible: Some indication this cannot be implemented. | 0 |
| | May or may not be feasible: Contradictory evidence this can be implemented. | 2 |
| | Probably feasible: Some indication this can be implemented. | 3 |
| | Definitely feasible: Can be implemented. | 3 |

Table 5.2. Governance Practices on Basel 1 2nd Round Data: Nonconsensus.

| Statement | Ratings | Total Number of Panelist Who Selected Each Ratings |
|---|---|---|
| Statement 12 – Governance practices senior bank managers can implement toward capital regulation that are effective in reducing losses entail adherence to the Basel principles around managing risk. | | |
| | Highly undesirable: Will have major negative effect. | 1 |
| | Undesirable: Will have a negative effect with little or no positive effect. | 0 |
| | Neither desirable nor undesirable: Will have equal positive and negative effects. | 3 |
| | Desirable: Will have a positive effect with minimum negative effects. | 2 |
| | Highly desirable: Will have a positive effect and little or no negative effect. | 1 |
| | Definitely infeasible: Cannot be implemented (unworkable). | 0 |
| | Probably infeasible: Some indication this cannot be implemented. | 0 |
| | May or may not be feasible: Contradictory evidence this can be implemented. | 2 |

*(Continued)*

Table 5.2. *(Continued)*

| Statement | Ratings | Total Number of Panelist Who Selected Each Ratings |
|---|---|---|
| | Probably feasible: Some indication this can be implemented. | 5 |
| | Definitely feasible: Can be implemented. | 5 |

Table 5.3. Compliance Practices on Test Measurements 2nd Round Data: Nonconsensus.

| Statement | Ratings | Total Number of Panelist Who Selected Each Ratings |
|---|---|---|
| Statement 16 – Compliance practices toward capital regulation that can reduce losses include tests that measure compliance with regulatory requirements. | | |
| | Highly undesirable: Will have major negative effect. | 1 |
| | Undesirable: Will have a negative effect with little or no positive effect. | 1 |
| | Neither desirable nor undesirable: Will have equal positive and negative effects. | 0 |
| | Desirable: Will have a positive effect with minimum negative effects. | 2 |

Table 5.3. *(Continued)*

| Statement | Ratings | Total Number of Panelist Who Selected Each Ratings |
|---|---|---|
| | Highly desirable: Will have a positive effect and little or no negative effect. | 3 |
| | Definitely infeasible: Cannot be implemented (unworkable). | 0 |
| | Probably infeasible: Some indication this cannot be implemented. | 0 |
| | May or may not be feasible: Contradictory evidence this can be implemented. | 1 |
| | Probably feasible: Some indication this can be implemented. | 4 |
| | Definitely feasible: Can be implemented. | 6 |

(2021) mentioned HSBC, UK, is a conduit/vehicle used for money laundering and was forced to pay US$1.9bn in a settlement for failure to prevent drug kings and rogue nations from using the bank to launder money. HSBC's inadequate Customer Due Diligence (CDD) on foreign correspondent account holder and ineffective AML program made it possible for traffickers/money launderers to process illegal activities across countries (Cuba, Iran, Libya) that are banned; HSBC forfeited $1.256 billion and $665 million civil penalties (Rathod, 2022). JP Morgan was found to be in violation of compliance rules relating undue favors and bribery which are considered to be criminal activities by regulators and paid settlement of $265 million (Rathod, 2022). Meral (2020) noted significant fines handed out to banks found to be not in compliance with AML legal requirements with charges increased from $26.6 million dollars as of 2011 to $3.5 billion as of 2012. These financial institutions (MoneyGram Inti, $100 million in 2012, First Bank of Delaware, $15 million for violating AML laws in 2012, TD Bank NA was charged for $37.5 million in 2013, JP Morgan Chase Bank charged for $461

Table 5.4. Internal Control Practices on Monitoring Assets 2nd Round Data: Nonconsensus.

| Statement | Ratings | Total Number of Panelist Who Selected Each Ratings |
|---|---|---|
| Statement 22 – Internal control activities toward capital regulation that can be effective in reducing losses include compliance and content monitoring of bank assets as well as complete overview of all activities. | | |
| | Undesirable: Will have a negative effect with little or no positive effect. | 1 |
| | Neither desirable nor undesirable: Will have equal positive and negative effects. | 1 |
| | Desirable: Will have a positive effect with minimum negative effects. | 2 |
| | Highly desirable: Will have a positive effect and little or no negative effect. | 2 |
| | Definitely infeasible: Cannot be implemented (unworkable). | 0 |
| | Probably infeasible: Some indication this cannot be implemented. | 0 |
| | May or may not be feasible: Contradictory evidence this can be implemented. | 2 |

Table 5.4. *(Continued)*

| Statement | Ratings | Total Number of Panelist Who Selected Each Ratings |
|---|---|---|
| | Probably feasible: Some indication this can be implemented. | 4 |
| | Definitely feasible: Can be implemented. | 5 |

Table 5.5. Governance Practices on Stress Tests 2nd Round Data: Nonconsensus.

| Statement | Ratings | Total Number of Panelist Who Selected Each Ratings |
|---|---|---|
| Statement 27 – Governance practices senior bank managers can implement toward capital regulation that are effective in reducing losses entail introduction of stress tests on vulnerable areas and assessment of the appropriateness of stress scenarios considered. | | |
| | Highly undesirable: Will have major negative effect. | 0 |
| | Undesirable: Will have a negative effect with little or no positive effect. | 1 |
| | Neither desirable nor undesirable: Will have equal positive and negative effects. | 1 |

*(Continued)*

Table 5.5. *(Continued)*

| Statement | Ratings | Total Number of Panelist Who Selected Each Ratings |
|---|---|---|
| | Desirable: Will have a positive effect with minimum negative effects. | 3 |
| | Highly desirable: Will have a positive effect and little or no negative effect. | 1 |
| | Definitely infeasible: Cannot be implemented (unworkable). | 0 |
| | Probably infeasible: Some indication this cannot be implemented. | 1 |
| | May or may not be feasible: Contradictory evidence this can be implemented. | 3 |
| | Probably feasible: Some indication this can be implemented. | 3 |
| | Definitely feasible: Can be implemented. | 4 |

million, ING bank paid $619) exorbitant fines relation to violations and deficiencies of AML compliance programs in 2014 (Meral, 2020).

ING is a Dutch bank fined $619 million by the US Government for violations of US sanctions against Cuba and Iran where the bank moved $1.6 billion illegally through the United States during 2007 by concealing the nature of the transactions (Mugarura, 2015). ING eliminated payment data that would have unmasked sanctioned countries and entities, advised clients how to evade computer filters which would have prevented sanctioned entities from gaining access to the US banking system, and provided US finance services to shell companies linked to sanctioned vessels (Mugarura, 2015). Lloyd Bank paid $350 million settle charges of changing client records for clients from sanctioned areas (Iran, Sudan) while Barclays Bank settled charges of £298 million for violating US rules for sanctioned countries (Mugarura, 2015). Money laundering and illegal

Table 5.6. Governance Practices on Model Validation 3rd Round Data: Nonconsensus.

| Statement | Ratings | Total Number of Panelist Who Selected Each Ratings |
|---|---|---|
| Statement 30 – Governance practices senior bank managers can implement toward capital regulation that are effective in reducing losses entail model validation and independent review (self-check/assessment). | | |
| | Highly undesirable: Will have major negative effect. | 0 |
| | Undesirable: Will have a negative effect with little or no positive effect. | 1 |
| | Neither desirable nor undesirable: Will have equal positive and negative effects. | 0 |
| | Desirable: Will have a positive effect with minimum negative effects. | 3 |
| | Highly desirable: Will have a positive effect and little or no negative effect. | 3 |
| | Definitely infeasible: Cannot be implemented (unworkable). | 0 |
| | Probably infeasible: Some indication this cannot be implemented. | 0 |
| | May or may not be feasible: Contradictory evidence this can be implemented. | 0 |

*(Continued)*

Table 5.6. *(Continued)*

| Statement | Ratings | Total Number of Panelist Who Selected Each Ratings |
|---|---|---|
| | Probably feasible: Some indication this can be implemented. | 5 |
| | Definitely feasible: Can be implemented. | 5 |

activities have led to the collapse of banks as stipulated by Johnson and Desmond (2002) in the mention of the collapse of the Bank of Credit and Commerce International (BCCI) relating to 9 Mexican banks' involvement in (laundering drug money) government execution of operation Casablanca. There are other banks such as Citibank's handling of its private accounts, Bank of New York's involvement in Russian mafia money laundering that reflects the relationship between banks, illegal activities, and linking the banking sector as a vehicle for laundering of funds (Johnson & Desmond Lim, 2002). Globalization of the banking sector and the liberalization of the market they function in have contributed to growing size of the money laundering problem laundered funds that range from US$300bn to US$1,000bn of which US$400bn a year came from illegal drug trade (Johnson & Desmond Lim, 2002). Indian banks during 2011–17 were involved with illegal activities (money laundering, terror financing, drug dealing, and financial frauds) as noted FinCEN's Suspicious Activity Report (SAR) where 44 Indian banks including branches of foreign banks operating in India received $482,181,226 from outside the country and transferred $406,278,962 (Ghosh, 2021). Bank of Baroda's weak AML framework and system controls prevented them to mitigate and act appropriately to 8,692 alerts that failed to dispose, and being unable to detect and report SAR, failed due diligence with 73 customer accounts, untimely filing of 8,822 Electronic Funds Transfer (EFT) reports (Ghosh, 2021). The inadequacies and failure to effectively meet the AML requirements led to Bank of Baroda being fined in 2018 by the Financial Intelligence Unit (FIU) for fraud involving US$ 900 million collusion between traders and bank officials in tax evasion schemes (Ghosh, 2021). Andrew (2021) stated western tax havens (Switzerland, Luxembourg, and Liechtenstein) are exploited by criminals to establish shell companies to store illicit funds; cases in Italy underscored the level of corruption and involvement of money laundering in the west. A case in Italy pointed to bribed judicial officials in Italy to influence a court decision and use of illegal bank accounts in countries (the United States,

Table 5.7. Governance Practices on Within Any Stress Test or Ratio
Guidelines 3rd Round Data: Nonconsensus.

| Statement | Ratings | Total Number of Panelist Who Selected Each Ratings |
|---|---|---|
| Statement 93 – Governance practices senior bank managers can implement toward capital regulation that are effective in reducing losses entail to be well within any stress test or ratio guidelines. | | |
| | Highly undesirable: Will have major negative effect. | 0 |
| | Undesirable: Will have a negative effect with little or no positive effect. | 1 |
| | Neither desirable nor undesirable: Will have equal positive and negative effects. | 1 |
| | Highly desirable: Will have a positive effect and little or no negative effect. | 5 |
| | Definitely infeasible: Cannot be implemented (unworkable). | 1 |
| | Probably infeasible: Some indication this cannot be implemented. | 0 |
| | May or may not be feasible: Contradictory evidence this can be implemented. | 1 |
| | Probably feasible: Some indication this can be implemented. | 6 |
| | Definitely feasible: Can be implemented. | 2 |

Singapore, Costa Rica, British Virgin Islands, Cook Islands) to launder and conceal traces of $400 million of tainted funds (Andrew, 2021).

Banks and financial institutions strive to prevent themselves from being exposed to receiving penalties due to the business risk exposure of where they transact business (high-risk countries, individuals, companies) that are susceptible to the risk of money laundering. Meral (2020) mentioned banks took to de-risking practices which entails mass customer exit programs, terminating business relationships to avoid money laundering which impacted local banks and money services negatively by forcing them out of business. This left many small countries being cut off from the global banking system and having to find alternative work around. For example, the Caribbean was severely affected with 69% of decline in Correspondent Banking Relationship terminations (Meral, 2020). Many first and second world countries that rely on aid sent through banks were impacted by banks withdrawing services for fear of violation of sanctions and money laundering laws and receiving penalties/punishment from regulators. Eckert (2021) argues financial institutions were unwilling to transfer funds into high-risk areas where humanitarian actors frequently operate, closed nonprofit organization (NPO) bank accounts, in some instances denied and/or delayed financial transfers. As such, the dire needs of people in areas in need of aid service by NGO were negatively impacted; Eckert (2021) mention humanitarian groups complain that business decisions made by banks to transfer funds are not based on needs but rather the logic was based on risk. Many NPO programs were terminated in high-risk money laundering and sanctions area; populations of individual in need of humanitarian assistance were denied critical aid (Eckert, 2020). Humanitarian actors have also witnessed increasing conditions and funding restrictions in the form of donors' contractual clauses in grant agreements, which have the effect of offloading risk onto NPOs. The following section explores these challenges in greater depth. Meral (2020) stated the core reason of de-risking is to comply with AML rules and mitigate the risk of noncompliance. Hence, small banks and money service businesses shift their transaction from regulated channels to unregulated channels (Meral, 2020). Barclays Bank Pic was penalize in 2010 and paid $298 million in 2010 for violations relating to high-risk areas (Iran, North Korea, Myanmar sanctioned areas of Sudan), and violations of Zimbabwe sanctions paid $2.5 million in 2016 (Meral, 2020).

Banks have argued that they lost their competitive edge because they had to cut back on business in some countries to meet AML regulations. Mugarura (2015) mentioned AML/combating the financing of terrorism (CFT) regulations impede financial institution from trading with low income, undocumented migrant groups that are conducting legitimate business. This condition is worsened by banks being involved on several occasions with transmitting funds to sanctioned countries like Iran (Mugarura, 2015). The Office of Foreign Assets Control (OFAC) implements and manages economic sanctions against countries and individuals/groups identified as terrorist or partake in narcotic activities; these sanctions can block economic assets of persons or countries and place restrictions on their trade (Meral, 2020).

# Chapter 6

# Bank Secrecy Act Anti-Money Laundering Compliance Practices – Ineffective Practices

Banks made over 125 comments and complaints regarding Bank Secrecy Act (BSA) of 1970 relating to currency transaction reporting (CTR) thresholds, suspicious activity reporting (SAR), Know Your Customer (KYC) requirements (DeMenno, 2020). Many banks believe the efforts, manpower, systems needed to track and report these events/activities are extremely costly, significant labor hours, and the volume of data are too much for them to keep up with making their efforts ineffective. BSA Anti-Money Laundering (AML) requirements have intensified in recent times to counteract the significant increase in money laundering activities; as such, CTR thresholds, SAR, response to 9/11 KYC requirements frequency and thresholds for reporting have received significant updates by the regulators (DeMenno, 2020). Banks which are unable to meet the compliance requirements are exposed to greater risks, as well as the possibility of being penalized by the regulators for noncompliance. Many banks looked to interbank sending of funds to meet some of the compliance requirements specified by the regulators, but this was not successful. The use of the Society for Worldwide Interbank Financial Telecommunications (SWIFT) to conduct business transactions within banks has met challenges. Banks reacted to the finding paid by HSBC $1.92 billion dollars to state authorities in 2012 as a form of sanctions (DeMenno, 2020). These banks implemented preventive, detective, and monitoring procedures to their KYC process. This is an attempt by some banks to use KYC Registry which collects information about their customers in international trade cross borders to provide information to the authorities when requested; information is transparent when shared through the SWIFT new KYC application (Meral, 2020). SWIFT is a cooperative system deemed to be safe/secure serving financial sector for 40 years that enables financial institutions (communicate with each other, transmit payment orders, issue letter of guarantees, letter of credits) through uniform SWIFT messages (Meral, 2020). The SWIFT network is used all over the world by banks, securities institutions, and corporate customers (Meral, 2020). This system if executed effectively should mitigate the use of money

Compliance and Financial Crime Risk in Banks, 65–73
Copyright © 2024 Sophia Beckett Velez
Published under exclusive licence by Emerald Publishing Limited
doi:10.1108/978-1-83549-041-920241006

laundering methods (smurfing, structuring, Shell banks, offshore centers, fake or shell corporations, dummy companies (companies which use cash), loan back (auto finance) system, exchange bureaus, casinos, false invoice/fictitious export, export cash) to disguise illegal acts (Meral, 2020). As such, it is important to launch anti-money laundering measures grouped into categories (KYC, list of suspects, identify the customer, other obligations banks/private finance institutions, etc.) globally to prevent drug smuggling, terrorism, and crimes (Meral, 2020). There are countries such as India, Ghosh (2021) stated, where the Reserve Bank of India (RBI) rolled out the following regulatory measures:

- identification and classification of fraud, reporting fraud, fraud risk management;
- cyber security framework;
- timely implementation of operational controls related to strengthening SWIFT program;
- prudential standards on income recognition, asset classification;
- KYC/AML standard.

In an effort to ensure banks take these anti-money laundering measures serious, RBI imposes monetary penalties as part of its enforcement function (Ghosh, 2021). A similar framework was launched in the United States which was received with some level of reluctancy and low levels of desirability to implement the recommended activities. The tables below reflect some of the voting on statements on KYC and cybersecurity statements Round 2 votes are displayed in Tables 6.1 – 6.4 (Velez, 2020).

Table 6.1. Internal Control Practices on Know Your Customer 2nd Round Data: Nonconsensus.

| Statement | Ratings | Total Number of Panelist Who Selected Each Ratings |
|---|---|---|
| Statement 95 – Internal control activities toward capital regulation that can be effective in reducing losses includes bank managers verifying know you customer guidelines to ensure all information is true and accurate. | | |
| | Highly undesirable: Will have major negative effect. | 0 |

Table 6.1. *(Continued)*

| Statement | Ratings | Total Number of Panelist Who Selected Each Ratings |
|---|---|---|
| | Undesirable: Will have a negative effect with little or no positive effect. | 1 |
| | Neither desirable nor undesirable: Will have equal positive and negative effects. | 1 |
| | Desirable: Will have a positive effect with minimum negative effects. | 2 |
| | Highly desirable: Will have a positive effect and little or no negative effect. | 3 |
| | Definitely infeasible: Cannot be implemented (unworkable). | 0 |
| | Probably infeasible: Some indication this cannot be implemented. | 1 |
| | May or may not be feasible: Contradictory evidence this can be implemented. | 1 |
| | Probably feasible: Some indication this can be implemented. | 5 |
| | Definitely feasible: Can be implemented. | 3 |

A significant number of banks moved from a manual face-to-face know your customer exercise KYC check to an automated process, which turned out to be ineffective (Demetri's & Angell, 2006). KYC process when done in person, banker asks questions directly to customer onsite and then assesses the customers behavior. If customers are open and transparent in sharing information and supporting

Table 6.2. Governance Practices on Program Revisions 2nd Round Data: Nonconsensus.

| Statement | Ratings | Total Number of Panelist Who Selected Each Ratings |
|---|---|---|
| Statement 101 – Governance practices senior bank managers can implement toward capital regulation that are effective in reducing losses entails revising Know Your Customers programs annually, while taking into account new federal regulations for the banking industry. | | |
| | Highly undesirable: Will have major negative effect. | 0 |
| | Undesirable: Will have a negative effect with little or no positive effect. | 1 |
| | Neither desirable nor undesirable: Will have equal positive and negative effects. | 0 |
| | Desirable: Will have a positive effect with minimum negative effects. | 2 |
| | Highly desirable: Will have a positive effect and little or no negative effect. | 3 |
| | Definitely infeasible: Cannot be implemented (unworkable). | 0 |
| | Probably infeasible: Some indication this cannot be implemented. | 2 |

Table 6.2. *(Continued)*

| Statement | Ratings | Total Number of Panelist Who Selected Each Ratings |
|---|---|---|
| | May or may not be feasible: Contradictory evidence this can be implemented. | 0 |
| | Probably feasible: Some indication this can be implemented. | 4 |
| | Definitely feasible: Can be implemented. | 2 |

Table 6.3. Compliance Practices on BSA Teams 2nd Round Data: Nonconsensus.

| Statement | Ratings | Total Number of Panelist Who Selected Each Ratings |
|---|---|---|
| Statement 117 – Compliance practices toward capital regulation that can be effective in reducing losses incudes ongoing training of all stakeholders relative to compliance rules and regulations including BSA teams, branch control teams, and cyber security teams. | | |
| | Highly undesirable: Will have major negative effect. | 0 |
| | Undesirable: Will have a negative effect with little or no positive effect. | 2 |

*(Continued)*

Table 6.3. *(Continued)*

| Statement | Ratings | Total Number of Panelist Who Selected Each Ratings |
|---|---|---|
| | Neither desirable nor undesirable: Will have equal positive and negative effects | 0 |
| | Desirable: Will have a positive effect with minimum negative effects. | 2 |
| | Highly desirable: Will have a positive effect and little or no negative effect. | 2 |
| | Definitely infeasible: Cannot be implemented (unworkable). | 1 |
| | Probably infeasible: Some indication this cannot be implemented. | 0 |
| | May or may not be feasible: Contradictory evidence this can be implemented. | 0 |
| | Probably feasible: Some indication this can be implemented. | 2 |
| | Definitely feasible: Can be implemented. | 6 |

documentation; this is a positive exercise for the banks KYC program. There are technological problems with AML software automated feature being unable to identify root cause in the patterns of human behavior; hence, the main design to track down and prosecute money launderers have failed because the human element has been removed from the process (Demetri's & Angell, 2006). The main root cause of the problem question is not asked as they are seen as awkward questions; instead, questions are phrased from a technological approach as if the technology works, the problems lie elsewhere, and the solution is to implement more technology (Demetri's & Angell, 2006). Because bank employees are fearful of the possibility of going to jail

Table 6.4. Governance Practices on Cyber Security 2nd Round Data: Nonconsensus.

| Statement | Ratings | Total Number of Panelist Who Selected Each Ratings |
|---|---|---|
| Statement 102 – Governance practices senior bank managers can implement toward capital regulation that are effective in reducing losses entails safeguard customer information through a robust cyber security program that is proactive. | | |
| | Highly undesirable: Will have major negative effect. | 0 |
| | Undesirable: Will have a negative effect with little or no positive effect. | 0 |
| | Neither desirable nor undesirable: Will have equal positive and negative effects. | 1 |
| | Desirable: Will have a positive effect with minimum negative effects. | 2 |
| | Highly desirable: Will have a positive effect and little or no negative effect. | 3 |
| | Definitely infeasible: Cannot be implemented (unworkable). | 0 |
| | Probably infeasible: Some indication this cannot be implemented. | 1 |
| | May or may not be feasible: Contradictory evidence this can be implemented. | 0 |

*(Continued)*

Table 6.4. *(Continued)*

| Statement | Ratings | Total Number of Panelist Who Selected Each Ratings |
|---|---|---|
| | Probably feasible: Some indication this can be implemented. | 6 |
| | Definitely feasible: Can be implemented. | 2 |

if KYC is not completed as part of due diligence, many bank employees go through the exercise as a check the box to show they completed/met the requirements. The robust preventative due diligence attention/focus is not applied to this exercise and more reliance is placed on the automated system results with lack of management judgment. AML and compliance regulations updates have caused banks fears to grow that they are exposed to being penalized with heavy fines and jail sentences for failure to prevent a money launderer from operating; to minimize the risk of occurrence, banks moved from face-to-face KYC checks to an automated process (Demetri's & Angell, 2006). The increase in scrutiny placed on transaction and investigation generated a significant number of doubtful entries that were filed as a Suspicious Transaction Report (STR); the increase in volumes of STR and the required reporting made it impossible for management reviews and the appropriate attention needed (Demetri's & Angell, 2006). The share volume of data generated as false positives alone posed as a detection risk. The more volume generated, the less focus and targeted review is performed, which makes it difficult for reviewers to identify a real issue at play. The manual nature of the execution of AML procedures could no longer be supported by manual reporting and analysis; instead, banks replaced this old manual process by implementing reporting on autopilot through the use of technology (Demetri's & Angell, 2006). This resulted in false positives were not reviewed causing the system to identify great number of transactions to be identified as positive feedback (Demetri's & Angell, 2006). The removal of the human factor causes more problems as that thorough process, critical thinking and review by management was removed from the process.

This increased the level of detection risk where true issues go undetected; true fraudulent and money laundering activities go undetected because they became buried in the forest of STRs. Demetri's and Angell (2006) mentioned there are complexities between the background technological systems/processes and human activity systems that were burdened with an information overload. These have been a concern for the British Banking Association (BBA) that the large volumes of so-called false positives in the AML software are clear lack of sophistication in the technological approach (Demetri's & Angell, 2006). Many major banks have migrated a significant portion of banking activities (deposits, withdrawals, funds transfers, payments, wires) to online banking which subject the bank to increase money laundering risks, cybercrimes, and difficulties in enforcing KYC rules. This major movement with online transaction has been incentivized as noted by Rifai and Tisnanta (2022) due to significant number (2.5 billion which is 40%) of the world population using the internet through connected devices which tripled from 13.4 billion in 2015 to 38.5 billion in 2020. Banks feel they have to keep up with the trends of the modern times of conducting and accessing business online through the use of the internet. However, online banking platform has been manipulated by cyber criminals to launder funds without being detected; they have used other avenues (e-gambling, online auctioning, cryptocurrency, digital payments methods) to bypass the AML laws (Rifai & Tisnanta, 2022). Bitcoin has been used in the international market to launder funds without detection as it lacks transparency of personal identification (no phone number, email address, or any other identifying information) of individual which cannot be stopped by authorities (Gladstein, 2021). Fantom users download software from the internet and transport money back and forth to individuals within minutes without government knowledge, no censorship, and without personal information (Gladstein, 2021). Government (FATF, FinCEN) may try to regulate the Bitcoin merchants by forcing them to enforce/adhere to KYC laws that would identify customers who wish to pay in bitcoin, thereby overriding the technological privacy benefits which could be nullified (Gladstein, 2021). These government stretched rules to cover the risk presented by Bitcoins through KYC provisions may provide major challenges for the growth of the bitcoin industry (Gladstein, 2021). Besides the use of Bitcoins, cyber criminals set on carrying out money laundering activities bye-pass laws and evade the law enforcement agencies though the use of hackers that manipulate and alter existing payment mechanisms into fraudulent method (Rifai & Tisnanta, 2022). Customers are concerned about the risk of their identity and account data falling in cyber criminals' hands. Banks are forced to allocate resources and time to the safeguard of customer information; Boora and Kavita (2018) mentioned important considerations that should be given by bank management to the use of risk management initiatives that may safeguard customer information through a robust cyber security program that is actively monitored. To achieve this objective, a strong technological infrastructure, data quality has to be at the forefront of considerations (Boora & Kavita, 2018). The various challenges the cyber criminals posed to banks, financial markets, and the lack of effectiveness in the regulatory bodies enforcement action bodies have resolved to banks being reactive by alerting customers when there is a breach on their accounts (Rifai & Tisnanta, 2022). Rifai and Tisnanta (2022) highlight it is important to control cybercriminals and there is a need for an existence of cybercrime money laundering response mechanism in banks to alert customers of risk and consistently strive for compliance of safety measures. The preventive measures have not worked thus far under KYC, SAR reporting, and cyber security; banks have to rely on workarounds that are detective control and monitoring nature to alert customers and cure any damages/losses customers incurred due to cyber criminals' activity.

Chapter 7

# Capital Requirements – Ineffective Practices

Capital requirements were highlighted as key risk mitigation measure that banks and systematically important financial institutions (SIFIs) need to sustain and survive in a financial crisis. The 2008 recession highlights banks' vulnerability, potential to become insolvent, causes bank runs, and cripples the global economy. Compliance measures highlighted in capital requirements were implemented by the regulators in Basel III and Dodd–Frank Wall Street Reform and Consumer Protection Act (DFA) in the United States in July 2010. Large banks are subject to mandatory Basel III Capital compliance measures that requires maintenance of larger proportion of bank capital as high quality and demonstrate this in their Comprehensive Capital Analysis and Review (CCAR) stress test filings (Wall, 2017). There are compliance guidance developed for banks to meet capital adequacy requirements as noted in Basel III (Boora & Kavita, 2018; Subsequent 2008), tier 1 capital requirements were set at a minimum of 3%, and banks who maintained tier 1 capital ratio above 6% were identified by the regulators as well capitalized (Herring, 2016). Basel III has higher tier 1 capital requirements with equity (common stock plus retained earnings), Common Equity Tier 1 (CET1) 4.5% of risk-weighted assets (RWAs), minimum tier 1 capital ratio from 4 to 6%, and capital conservation buffer of 2.5% of RWAs (Baker et al., 2017). Subsequent to the Basel III announcements, OCC made changes to risk weights of the Advanced Approach system made updates to the market risk rule to exclude credit rating–based risk assessment, introduced additional capital rules, bank capital levels increases, create a Capital Conservation Buffer, and required banks to have additional capital beyond required levels in order to pay dividends (Hogan, 2021). Banks may be incentivized to take on more risky activities by risk-based capital (RBC) ratios requirements that tend to increase banks compliance cost due to their nature to be complex; the increased in their budgetary costs relating to regulatory agencies may cause increase in high-risk behavior. Furthermore, RBC ratios have been dubbed as ineffective at predicting bank risk (Hogan & Meredith, 2016). This has been reinforced by Dowd and Hutchinson's (2016) views on capital ratio requirements, RWA, and stress testing

Compliance and Financial Crime Risk in Banks, 75–88
Copyright © 2024 Sophia Beckett Velez
Published under exclusive licence by Emerald Publishing Limited
doi:10.1108/978-1-83549-041-920241007

of capital has been ineffective; there are situations where bankers decapitalize their own banks and then pass their risk-taking cost to the taxpayers.

It has been noted that this capital ratio requirements established through Basel III didn't deter senior bank managers from taking advantage of loopholes within the regulatory landscape and exploiting arbitrage opportunities (Petitjean, 2013). It is within the bank's nature to take on excessive risk which is endogenous to regulations (Petitjean, 2013). Banks found a way to transfer risk from their balance sheet to capital markets which has been short-term beneficial to the bank (Le et al., 2016). Many banks saw the capital requirements as an over-regulation which accelerated their risk-taking activities, and many came up with financial innovation activities aimed at circumventing regulation (Petitjean, 2013). One of the circumventing tool banks used is securitization, which enabled them to grow loan portfolios which would have been hindered by banking book capital requirements (Hanke & Sekerke, 2017). Banks use securitization tools which involve transferring balance sheet assets to a special purpose vehicle which is financed through the issuance of securities to outside investors (Le et al., 2016). The voting results on compliance activities relating to capital requirements deemed ineffective by the panel of expert statements Round 2 votes are displayed below Tables 7.1–7.9 (Velez, 2020).

Table 7.1. Compliance Practices on Test Measures 2nd Round Data: Nonconsensus.

| Statement | Ratings | Total Number of Panelist Who Selected Each Ratings |
|---|---|---|
| Statement 16 - Compliance practices toward capital regulation that can reduce losses include tests that measure compliance with regulatory requirements. | | |
| | Highly undesirable: Will have major negative effect. | 2 |
| | Undesirable: Will have a negative effect with little or no positive effect. | 0 |
| | Neither desirable nor undesirable: Will have equal positive and negative effects. | 1 |
| | Desirable: Will have a positive effect with minimum negative effects. | 4 |

Table 7.1. *(Continued)*

| Statement | Ratings | Total Number of Panelist Who Selected Each Ratings |
|---|---|---|
| | Highly desirable: Will have a positive effect and little or no negative effect. | 4 |
| | Definitely infeasible: Cannot be implemented (unworkable). | 1 |
| | Probably infeasible: Some indication this cannot be implemented. | 1 |
| | May or may not be feasible: Contradictory evidence this can be implemented. | 1 |
| | Probably feasible: Some indication this can be implemented. | 2 |
| | Definitely feasible: Can be implemented. | 5 |

Table 7.2. Compliance Practices on Communication 2nd Round Data: Nonconsensus.

| Statement | Ratings | Total Number of Panelist Who Selected Each Ratings |
|---|---|---|
| Statement 59 - Compliance practices toward capital regulation that can be effective in reducing losses include establishing and communicating compliance policy across pertinent organizations. | | |

*(Continued)*

Table 7.2. *(Continued)*

| Statement | Ratings | Total Number of Panelist Who Selected Each Ratings |
|---|---|---|
| | Highly undesirable: Will have major negative effect. | 1 |
| | Undesirable: Will have a negative effect with little or no positive effect. | 2 |
| | Neither desirable nor undesirable: Will have equal positive and negative effects. | 1 |
| | Desirable: Will have a positive effect with minimum negative effects. | 3 |
| | Highly desirable: Will have a positive effect and little or no negative effect. | 5 |
| | Definitely infeasible: Cannot be implemented (unworkable). | 0 |
| | Probably infeasible: Some indication this cannot be implemented. | 0 |
| | May or may not be feasible: Contradictory evidence this can be implemented. | 1 |
| | Probably feasible: Some indication this can be implemented. | 7 |
| | Definitely feasible: Can be implemented. | 2 |

Table 7.3. Compliance Practices on Compliance Risks 2nd Round Data: Nonconsensus.

| Statement | Ratings | Total Number of Panelist Who Selected Each Ratings |
|---|---|---|
| Statement 60 - Compliance practices toward capital regulation that can be effective in reducing losses include identification of compliance risks and controls at the relevant organizational level. | | |
| | Highly undesirable: Will have major negative effect. | 0 |
| | Undesirable: Will have a negative effect with little or no positive effect. | 2 |
| | Neither desirable nor undesirable: Will have equal positive and negative effects. | 2 |
| | Desirable: Will have a positive effect with minimum negative effects. | 2 |
| | Highly desirable: Will have a positive effect and little or no negative effect. | 5 |
| | Definitely infeasible: Cannot be implemented (unworkable). | 0 |
| | Probably infeasible: Some indication this cannot be implemented. | 1 |
| | May or may not be feasible: Contradictory evidence. | 1 |
| | Probably feasible: Some indication this can be implemented. | 2 |
| | Definitely feasible: Can be implemented. | 6 |

Table 7.4. Compliance Practices on Remediation 2nd Round Data: Nonconsensus.

| Statement | Ratings | Total Number of Panelist Who Selected Each Ratings |
|---|---|---|
| Statement 61 - Compliance practices toward capital regulation that can be effective in reducing losses ensure compliance function is adhered to with clarity of responsibilities and remediation steps for breaches are discovered. | | |
| | Highly undesirable: Will have major negative effect. | 0 |
| | Undesirable: Will have a negative effect with little or no positive effect. | 0 |
| | Neither desirable nor undesirable: Will have equal positive and negative effects. | 1 |
| | Desirable: Will have a positive effect with minimum negative effects. | 4 |
| | Highly desirable: Will have a positive effect and little or no negative effect. | 5 |
| | Definitely infeasible: Cannot be implemented (unworkable). | 0 |
| | Probably infeasible: Some indication this cannot be implemented. | 1 |
| | May or may not be feasible: Contradictory evidence this can be implemented. | 1 |

Table 7.4. *(Continued)*

| Statement | Ratings | Total Number of Panelist Who Selected Each Ratings |
|---|---|---|
| | Probably feasible: Some indication this can be implemented. | 3 |
| | Definitely feasible: Can be implemented. | 5 |

Table 7.5. Compliance Practices on Periodic Assessment 2nd Round Data: Nonconsensus.

| Statement | Ratings | Total Number of Panelist Who Selected Each Ratings |
|---|---|---|
| Statement 63 - Compliance practices toward capital regulation that can be effective in reducing losses include periodic assessment of issues and issues closures. | | |
| | Highly undesirable: Will have major negative effect. | 0 |
| | Undesirable: Will have a negative effect with little or no positive effect. | 1 |
| | Neither desirable nor undesirable: Will have equal positive and negative effects. | 1 |
| | Highly desirable: Will have a positive effect and little or no negative effect. | 5 |
| | Definitely infeasible: Cannot be implemented (unworkable). | 1 |

*(Continued)*

Table 7.5. *(Continued)*

| Statement | Ratings | Total Number of Panelist Who Selected Each Ratings |
|---|---|---|
| | Probably infeasible: Some indication this cannot be implemented. | 1 |
| | May or may not be feasible: Contradictory evidence this can be implemented. | 1 |
| | Probably feasible: Some indication this can be implemented. | 2 |
| | Definitely feasible: Can be implemented. | 5 |

Table 7.6. Compliance Practices on Upper Management 2nd Round Data: Nonconsensus.

| Statement | Ratings | Total Number of Panelist Who Selected Each Ratings |
|---|---|---|
| Statement 64 - Compliance practices toward capital regulation that can be effective in reducing losses include reporting of compliance to upper management so they can make informed decisions on compliance risks. | | |
| | Highly undesirable: Will have major negative effect. | 0 |
| | Undesirable: Will have a negative effect with little or no positive effect. | 1 |

Table 7.6. *(Continued)*

| Statement | Ratings | Total Number of Panelist Who Selected Each Ratings |
|---|---|---|
| | Neither desirable nor undesirable: Will have equal positive and negative effects. | 1 |
| | Desirable: Will have a positive effect with minimum negative effects. | 4 |
| | Highly desirable: Will have a positive effect and little or no negative effect. | 4 |
| | Definitely infeasible: Cannot be implemented (unworkable). | 0 |
| | Probably infeasible: Some indication this cannot be implemented. | 0 |
| | May or may not be feasible: Contradictory evidence this can be implemented. | 2 |
| | Probably feasible: Some indication this can be implemented. | 3 |
| | Definitely feasible: Can be implemented. | 5 |

Table 7.7. Compliance Practices on Internal Control 2nd Round Data: Nonconsensus.

| Statement | Ratings | Total Number of Panelist Who Selected Each Ratings |
|---|---|---|
| Statement 100 - Compliance practices toward capital regulation that can be effective in reducing losses include internal controls utilized at every level to ensure potential liabilities are eliminated. | | |
| | Highly undesirable: Will have major negative effect. | 0 |
| | Undesirable: Will have a negative effect with little or no positive effect. | 1 |
| | Neither desirable nor undesirable: Will have equal positive and negative effects. | 4 |
| | Desirable: Will have a positive effect with minimum negative effects. | 3 |
| | Highly desirable: Will have a positive effect and little or no negative effect. | 3 |
| | Definitely infeasible: Cannot be implemented (unworkable). | 1 |
| | Probably infeasible: Some indication this cannot be implemented. | 3 |
| | May or may not be feasible: Contradictory evidence this can be implemented. | 1 |

Table 7.7. *(Continued)*

| Statement | Ratings | Total Number of Panelist Who Selected Each Ratings |
|---|---|---|
| | Probably feasible: Some indication this can be implemented. | 3 |
| | Definitely feasible: Can be implemented. | 1 |

Table 7.8. Compliance Practices on Training 2nd Round Data: Nonconsensus.

| Statement | Ratings | Total Number of Panelist Who Selected Each Ratings |
|---|---|---|
| Statement 128 - Compliance practices toward capital regulation that can be effective in reducing losses include ongoing training of all stakeholders relative to compliance rules and regulations including BSA teams, branch control teams, and cyber security teams. | | |
| | Highly undesirable: Will have major negative effect. | 0 |
| | Undesirable: Will have a negative effect with little or no positive effect. | 1 |
| | Neither desirable nor undesirable: Will have equal positive and negative effects. | 4 |
| | Desirable: Will have a positive effect with minimum negative effects. | 5 |

*(Continued)*

Table 7.8. *(Continued)*

| Statement | Ratings | Total Number of Panelist Who Selected Each Ratings |
|---|---|---|
| | Highly desirable: Will have a positive effect and little or no negative effect. | 2 |
| | Definitely infeasible: Cannot be implemented (unworkable). | 0 |
| | Probably infeasible: Some indication this cannot be implemented. | 0 |
| | May or may not be feasible: Contradictory evidence this can be implemented. | 4 |
| | Probably feasible: Some indication this can be implemented. | 2 |
| | Definitely feasible: Can be implemented. | 2 |

Table 7.9. Governance Practices on Vulnerable Areas 2nd Round Data: Nonconsensus.

| Statement | Ratings | Total Number of Panelist Who Selected Each Ratings |
|---|---|---|
| Statement 27 - Governance practices senior bank managers can implement toward capital regulation that are effective in reducing losses entail introduction of stress tests on vulnerable areas and assessment of the appropriateness of stress scenarios considered. | | |

Table 7.9. *(Continued)*

| Statement | Ratings | Total Number of Panelist Who Selected Each Ratings |
|---|---|---|
| | Highly undesirable: Will have major negative effect. | 0 |
| | Undesirable: Will have a negative effect with little or no positive effect. | 1 |
| | Neither desirable nor undesirable: Will have equal positive and negative effects. | 1 |
| | Desirable: Will have a positive effect with minimum negative effects. | 4 |
| | Highly desirable: Will have a positive effect and little or no negative effect. | 4 |
| | Definitely infeasible: Cannot be implemented (unworkable). | 0 |
| | Probably infeasible: Some indication this cannot be implemented. | 1 |
| | May or may not be feasible: Contradictory evidence this can be implemented. | 3 |
| | Probably feasible: Some indication this can be implemented. | 3 |
| | Definitely feasible: Can be implemented. | 3 |

The use of stress test to demonstrate compliance with the capital requirements has been rejected by many banks. Banks complete the stress test; however, their management are not supportive of this process. Dowd and Hutchinson (2016) maintained capital ratio requirements and stress testing of capital through use of federal regulators risk models has been ineffective. The independent stress test of selected bank capital performed to assess banks compliance by the Federal Reserve System (Fed) found several failing to meet the guideline. Fed stress test of banks in 2015 found Bank of America capital levels lower than expected, and they were asked to raise capital levels and resubmit their capital plans costing the bank $100 million (Walker et al., 2017). Citigroup spent $180 million in 2014 for the preparation of its submission, Morgan Stanley was asked to revise their capital plan for 2016, Deutsche Bank and Santander US failed the tests, and dividends restrictions were imposed by the Fed (Walker et al., 2017). The suggestion of having tests that measure compliance with regulatory requirements was not viewed favorably by banks. The compliance requirements posed through capital regulation were not accepted with open arms because of its negative impacts on banks. Hogan (2021) mentioned RBC has been impacting banks negatively and which has been understated or ignored. The Dodd–Frank Act 2010 (DFA) requirements for large banks classified as SIFIs to mitigate systemic risk the regulation created incentives for banks to downsize (Allen et al., 2016). The direct link of DFA requirement effecting shrinkage of SIFIs is unclear as there are instances where large organizations are growing larger (Allen et al., 2016). However, in some scenarios, SIFIs that are Bank Holding Companies (BHCs) have unpleasant results where they are forced to refile credit risk as market risk (Hanke & Sekerke, 2017). BHCs refile risk related to credit as market risk through use of transactions, commercial bank business as broker–dealer business, and create money through new lending avenues that are abusive (Hanke & Sekerke, 2017). The wins regulators' intended restrictions securitization was looking to garner had unintended results (Hanke & Sekerke, 2017).

There are challenges posed by abusive high-frequency trading practices to meeting capital requirements in banks, lack of market transparency, fair trade, accountability at the top, and conflicts of interest expose investors to unnecessary risks and fees (Barr, 2017). Banks have bypassed the capital requirements and taken to the use of off-balance sheet derivatives that are over-the-counter traded and not traded on organized exchanges, which have caused layers of regulatory problems (Mohamed, 2015). Banks have engaged in risky off-balance-sheet activities when on-balance-sheet assets become less profitable due to lower interest rates (Chang & Talley, 2017). Many large banks invest in high-risk off-balance-sheet assets to boost earning, increase the amount of higher risk assets in anticipation of higher expected return associated with them during the low interest rate periods (Chang & Talley, 2017). SIFI banks have engaged in extending leveraged activities to stay abreast of competition, through financial innovation and the use of off-balance-sheet trades leading to expansion available credit (Hale Balseven, 2016). Basel III leverage ratio of 3% of nonweighted assets is widely seen as very weak constraint on bank risk seeking (Hale Balseven, 2016). Banks trying to meet capital requirements as a compliance measure of regulatory laws is a risk they continuously face.

# Chapter 8

# Training

The importance of training employees and stakeholders at all levels within the bank has been highlighted after the continuous passing of new compliance laws and the severity of risk exposure stemming from lack of knowledge. Training helps bank stakeholders both at senior and junior level stay abreast of the new rules and law requirements in a fast-passed challenging, evolving, and heavily regulated financial services environment. Boora and Kavita (2018) highlight the importance of training in keeping up with the requirements of Basel III norms and the need for employees to upgrade their skills by participating in continuous compliance subject matter training pertaining to these new laws. Helena and Madsen (2021) assert compliance employees maintain their knowledge through ongoing training. The importance of collaboration with the regulators on compliance requirements and obtaining technical support from the regulators can assist in the achievement of effective Basel III compliance (Boora & Kavita, 2018). Similarly, Duncan (2021) reinforced the need for training at all levels through the organization (all employees, specific positions, board directors, internal and external stakeholders) with specific attention given to whom and how the training is provided. Duncan (2021) asserts the need for employee training maintained with evidence of current anti-money laundering (AML) certification from a recognized organization. There is also the need for monitoring and enforcement of training that will prevent employees from being tempted to not participate in the required trainings; this will minimize the possibilities of employees not possessing current certification is the banks and require them to renew these certifications timely (Duncan, 2021). There are human resources (HR) controls that can be implemented to prevent employees from not participating in training and ensuring mandatory trainings are adhered to. Training has been identified as one of the important mitigating tools that can be used to lower high-risk compliance areas while meeting the mandatory regulatory requirement set by international government regulators. Training as a tool is valuable when there is measurement of its performance are put in place namely: monitoring, preventative and detective training activities.

There are detective and monitoring controls that are designed to identify employees/individuals who are required to participate in training and have failed to do so. Monitoring controls are reporting in nature and tend to reinforce the preventative and detective controls as the results of these performance controls are reported in the monthly and quarterly reporting results of the monitoring controls report. Duncan (2021) mentioned that HR department can track training and

Compliance and Financial Crime Risk in Banks, 89–96

Copyright © 2024 Sophia Beckett Velez

Published under exclusive licence by Emerald Publishing Limited

doi:10.1108/978-1-83549-041-920241008

certification through HR controls which is reinforced by certifications such as Financial Intermediary and Broker Association (FIBA) and Association of Certified Anti-Money Laundering Specialist (ACAMS) alerting employees via emails of upcoming renewal dates, webinars, and other available training. The status of employee's participation can be tracked online, and employees are held accountable for maintaining their AML certification (Duncan, 2021). The lack of compliance in maintaining current certifications can expose an employee to being penalized by the banks and the possibility of being terminated. There is emphasis on specialty training need to be provided for various employees based on the department and products they work with. Ghosh (2021) mentioned bank employees should receive specialty training on banking risk issues and in particular on various RBI circulars; this could play an important risk mitigation function in improving weak compliance activities. These trainings can be intensive and conducive to the compliance environment, which resolve challenges encountered from technological changes, legal environment, and ethical problems (Ghosh, 2021). The voting results on training by the panel of expert statements Round 2 votes are displayed below Tables 8.1–8.4 (Velez, 2020).

Table 8.1. Internal Control Practices on Prioritize Training 2nd Round Data: Nonconsensus.

| Statement | Ratings | Total Number of Panelist Who Selected Each Ratings |
|---|---|---|
| Statement 84 – Internal control activities toward capital regulation that can be effective in reducing losses include making training a priority. | | |
| | Highly undesirable: Will have major negative effect. | 0 |
| | Undesirable: Will have a negative effect with little or no positive effect. | 0 |
| | Neither desirable nor undesirable: Will have equal positive and negative effects. | 0 |
| | Desirable: Will have a positive effect with minimum negative effects. | 3 |
| | Highly desirable: Will have a positive effect and little or no negative effect. | 6 |

Table 8.1. *(Continued)*

| Statement | Ratings | Total Number of Panelist Who Selected Each Ratings |
|---|---|---|
| | Definitely infeasible: Cannot be implemented (unworkable). | 1 |
| | Probably infeasible: Some indication this cannot be implemented. | 0 |
| | May or may not be feasible: Contradictory evidence this can be implemented. | 1 |
| | Probably feasible: Some indication this can be implemented. | 4 |
| | Definitely feasible: Can be implemented. | 5 |

Table 8.2. Risk Management Practices on Training Employees 2nd Round Data: Nonconsensus.

| Statement | Ratings | Total Number of Panelist Who Selected Each Ratings |
|---|---|---|
| Statement 104 – Risk management practices toward capital regulation that can be effective in reducing losses include having frequent training of employers to ensure adherence to banking industry rules and regulations. | | |
| | Highly undesirable: Will have major negative effect. | 0 |

*(Continued)*

Table 8.2. *(Continued)*

| Statement | Ratings | Total Number of Panelist Who Selected Each Ratings |
|---|---|---|
| | Undesirable: Will have a negative effect with little or no positive effect. | 0 |
| | Neither desirable nor undesirable: Will have equal positive and negative effects. | 1 |
| | Desirable: Will have a positive effect with minimum negative effects. | 2 |
| | Highly desirable: Will have a positive effect and little or no negative effect. | 3 |
| | Definitely infeasible: Cannot be implemented (unworkable). | 0 |
| | Probably infeasible: Some indication this cannot be implemented. | 1 |
| | May or may not be feasible: Contradictory evidence this can be implemented. | 2 |
| | Probably feasible: Some indication this can be implemented. | 3 |
| | Definitely feasible: Can be implemented. | 3 |

Training of all stakeholders, frequently, thoroughly and making this a priority have been a recurring theme throughout the statements voted on relating to training. It is important to note that training should begin from the onset when a new employee starts with the bank. That mindset of training should be reinforced from the moment the individual starts their role at the bank. The onboarding

Table 8.3. Assurance Practices on Thorough Training 2nd Round Data: Nonconsensus.

| Statement | Ratings | Total Number of Panelist Who Selected Each Ratings |
|---|---|---|
| Statement 111 – Assurance practices toward capital regulation that can be effective in reducing losses include through training of staff. | | |
| | Highly undesirable: Will have major negative effect. | 0 |
| | Undesirable: Will have a negative effect with little or no positive effect. | 1 |
| | Neither desirable nor undesirable: Will have equal positive and negative effects. | 1 |
| | Desirable: Will have a positive effect with minimum negative effects. | 3 |
| | Highly desirable: Will have a positive effect and little or no negative effect. | 6 |
| | Definitely infeasible: Cannot be implemented (unworkable). | 1 |
| | Probably infeasible: Some indication this cannot be implemented. | 0 |
| | May or may not be feasible: Contradictory evidence this can be implemented. | 0 |
| | Probably feasible: Some indication this can be implemented. | 5 |
| | Definitely feasible: Can be implemented. | 3 |

Table 8.4. Compliance Practices on Cyber Security Teams 2nd Round Data: Nonconsensus.

| Statement | Ratings | Total Number of Panelist Who Selected Each Ratings |
|---|---|---|
| Statement 128 – Compliance practices toward capital regulation that can be effective in reducing losses include ongoing training of all stakeholders relative to compliance rules and regulations including BSA teams, branch control teams, and cyber security teams. | | |
| | Highly undesirable: Will have major negative effect. | 0 |
| | Undesirable: Will have a negative effect with little or no positive effect. | 1 |
| | Neither desirable nor undesirable: Will have equal positive and negative effects. | 4 |
| | Desirable: Will have a positive effect with minimum negative effects. | 5 |
| | Highly desirable: Will have a positive effect and little or no negative effect. | 2 |
| | Definitely infeasible: Cannot be implemented (unworkable). | 0 |
| | Probably infeasible: Some indication this cannot be implemented. | 0 |
| | May or may not be feasible: Contradictory | 4 |

Table 8.4. *(Continued)*

| Statement | Ratings | Total Number of Panelist Who Selected Each Ratings |
|---|---|---|
| | evidence this can be implemented. | |
| | Probably feasible: Some indication this can be implemented. | 2 |
| | Definitely feasible: Can be implemented. | 2 |

process for new employees should be followed up with the employment relationship and development facilitated through ongoing training that is carried by having a well-prepared training plan that includes all employees of the firm (Helena & Madsen, 2021). The bank's routines need to be executed in a manner where the processes are completed in accordance with relevant laws and regulations; training employees helps in meeting this obligation and gaining understanding of the process (Helena & Madsen, 2021). The bank's compliance function conducts follow-up checks on employees' performance in accordance to established processes which leads to recommendation of training for employees with additional individual follow-up (Helena & Madsen, 2021). The lack of adherence to compliance activities and reporting to the chief compliance officer is reinforced through having a whistleblowing program. Ghosh (2021) asserts the company should strengthen the mechanism of whistleblowing, protect the whistleblower, offer empowerment to risk management department and other areas that support the success of the Chief Compliance Officer (CCO). There is a need for fully trained network administrators to facilitate the execution of many of the legal requirements banks are required to execute namely: financial units to set up cybersecurity units, risk departments, fraud prevention units, BSA/AML management boards, AML intelligence units, AML analysts/investigators (Rifai & Tisnanta, 2022). Bank personnel who have the function of working with AML transactions can receive training provided by legislators that will sharpen their skills and awareness to timely detect offences and suspected money laundering (Rifai & Tisnanta, 2022). There are tools available online that employees can use to train on a particular subject matter that will provide wide scale to global cybercrime awareness; one being the Budapest Convention on Cybercrime 2001 international treaty emphasis on cybercrimes committed via the internet and other computer networks, which can help familiarize employees with these types of possible threats (Rifai & Tisnanta, 2022).

There are scenarios where banks can be sued for harm incurred on other parties because the bank did not have or failed to demonstrate they have an effective training program. Mugarura (2015) mentioned investigations into several Mexican banks regarding money laundering schemes and one in particular Banco Mercantil del Norte faced a lawsuit based on failure to have policies and AML strategy. Banco Mercantil del Norte faced a US$ 7 million claim brought on by the US Government based on the bank failure to operate a comprehensive AML strategy and policies; the bank defended itself against this claim and was successful in doing so (Mugarura, 2015). It should be noted that part of the US Government claim against Banco Mercantil del Norte was the lack of an effective training program for its staff. Mugarura (2015) states the bank did not have a clear policy on the training and education of staff at various levels, the lack of evidence of distribution of manual to employees on the prevention of money laundering at mid and higher level. The deficiencies in the training program were evidence in lack of comprehensive Mexico-wide training policies of banks staff (Mugarura, 2015). Helena and Madsen (2021) noted compliance as a function in on organizations works when it is socialized throughout the company will be more effective and have less communication gaps and lowers control risks. The changes within an organization that impact compliance functions and the control environment can be effective through training; this organizational change could be implemented through structural changes in job roles and training which is impactful to skills and methods (Helena & Madsen, 2021).

Part 3

# Compliance Environment and Effective Leadership Practices

# Chapter 9

# Sanctions

Banks have to ensure they do not violate the various levels of sanctions imposed by international governments; in the United States, sanctions are imposed on countries, companies, and individuals that banks are prohibited from conducting business. US sanctions are enforced through heavy liabilities on offenders found guilty and liable for committing a civil violation of sanctions (Eckert, 2021). Iran received sanctions and blacklisted by the Financial Action Task Force (FATF) because they were unwilling to agree to two international conventions for Palermo and Anti-Terrorist Financing Conventions which are relevant to combat crime (Vahid et al., 2021). A country that is blacklisted can suffer reputational damage among investors which has knock on effects where there could be pressure to comply to prevent loss of capital (Vahid et al., 2021). Sanctions should be documented and maintained as part of the recordkeeping process with some mention of maintaining these records in the enterprise-wide risk assessment (EWRA) methodology oversee by the board or risk committee (Duncan, 2021). Meral (2020) stated Office of Foreign Assets Control (OFAC) monitoring function as an agency entails the implementation and managing of economic sanctions against countries and individuals/groups who are terrorist or partake in narcotic activities. Sanctions are used as an effective tool and activity to block economic assets of persons and countries and restrict their trade with other parties (Meral, 2020).

Meral (2020) highlights the role of OFAC in being the publisher and maintenance of the list of Specially Designated Nationals (SDN) and Blocked Persons List available on a web page accessible to banks, citizens, and for the general public knowledge. The OFAC list consists of companies and individuals acting on behalf of targeted countries, restricted countries, terrorists, and narcotics smugglers (Meral, 2020). The US government required detected parties and countries on this sanction list assets blocked; the Trade with the Enemy Act (TWEA) Law states that US citizens are prohibited from dealing with entities, parties, or countries on this prohibited list (Meral, 2020). Campbell-Verduyn (2018) asserts the America war on terrorism and money laundering is frequently commingled with terrorist financing. The global community pulls its resources together and capabilities to mobilize a force to combat money laundering and terrorism financing; these efforts are met

Compliance and Financial Crime Risk in Banks, 99–105
Copyright © 2024 Sophia Beckett Velez
Published under exclusive licence by Emerald Publishing Limited
doi:10.1108/978-1-83549-041-920241009

with many challenges that lie within the banking sector (Kerimov et al., 2020). The banking sector is one of the significant conduits use to transfer/move funds which is a burden for regulators to counter the legalization of income; most terrorist actors' schemes of legalizing income at various stages use banks as intermediaries in the transfer of funds (Kerimov et al., 2020). There is a direct relationship between corruption and terrorist funding. Meral (2020) states when corruption increases, there is also an increase in corruption terrorism finance and drug trafficking and will increase money laundering mostly used for financing terrorism. September 11 terrorist attack heightened the importance of preventing money laundering, and anti-sentiments (illegal, dirty money created from illegal activities, terrorism finance) were enforced through the use of rolling out sanctions to prevent money laundering (Meral, 2020). There are established reputable international organizations (World Bank, United Nations, European union) that must get onboard with avoiding being parties to money laundering and must work cooperatively with other countries for the success of anti-money laundering (AML) initiatives (Meral, 2020). The critical nature of the issue at hand in being able to stop terrorism was highlighted in the 1998 bombings of US embassies in East Africa which was met with the response from the United Nations Security Council (UNSC) imposing sanctions on the Taliban and Al-Qaeda and their associated groups to deter international terrorism (Eckert, 2021).

The UNSC sanctions met pushed back and the Taliban's refused to turn over Osama bin Laden to face prosecution, hosting of training, and providing sanctuary for international terrorist groups (Eckert, 2021). Further measures were taken by the government effected where the council adopted Resolution 126719 in October 1999 which freeze assets and an aviation ban on the Taliban; these respective measures adopted under Chapter VII of the UN Charter allowed the government under international law to bind all their member states to enforce/ abide by these sanction activities (Eckert, 2021). The follow-up terrorist attacks on September 11, 2001 reflect the critical nature for sanctions used as an effective measure to mitigate terrorist activity, and this promulgated an evolution of UN sanctions; there were significant expansion of the 1267 sanctions, creation of the Counter-Terrorism Committee pursuant to UNSC Resolution 1373, emphasis placed on preventing the financing of terrorism activities by rolling out new adoption of domestic legislation, and stringent activities adopted by member states (Eckert, 2021). Johnson and Desmond Lim (2002) stated the September 11 attack on the United States forced governments to take a serious stance on the threat of terrorism to a country's democracy and financial stability. Bieler (2022) asserts in response to September 11, 2001, terrorist actions, the Patriot Act of 2001 was passed which amended and strengthened the Bank Secrecy Act's (BSA's) compliance program to include control activities; customer identification regimes, Know Your Customer (KYC), Customer Identification Program (CIP), customer due diligence (CDD), identify suspected terrorist activity, and maintained the supporting documentation/evidence as required by the regulators. This type of scrutiny and due diligence should be performed at the onset of opening bank accounts (Bieler, 2022).

Banks should be aware of individuals/entities associated with Al-Qaeda, including the Islamic State in Iraq in 2015, restricting targets from gaining access to resources (funds, people, commodities, etc.) and other dangerous behaviors (Eckert, 2021). Banks are required to impose these sanctions as part of the preventative, detective, and monitoring compliance due diligence activities. Meral (2020) asserts banks should take actions and precautionary measures to be in compliance with the international rules and to avoid sanction violations which is very important. Similarly, the Basel Committee echoed the importance of applying international standards rules and precautionary measures (online sanctions screens, KYC, FATF Forty Recommendations, invest for technologic, SWIFT sanctions screening) to prevent AML and terrorist finance occurrences (Meral, 2020). Campbell-Verduyn (2018) stated there are concerns put forth by the International Monetary Fund (IMF) that cryptocurrency when used by terrorist can conceal pertinent nature of transactions inclusive illicit origin, sanctioned destination of funds, thereby making possible for the illegal money laundering to take place. Meral (2020) mentioned banks have been found to be not in compliance with AML laws and they receive sanctions and punishments. The charges from sanctions and punishments went from $26.6 million dollars in 2011 to $3.5 billion 2012; many institutions (MoneyGram Inti $100 million in 2012, First Bank of Delaware $15 million for violating AML laws in 2012, TD Bank NA $37.5 million in 2013, JP Morgan Chase Bank charged $461 million for violations and deficiencies of AML compliance programs in 2014, Courts & Company pay charges totaling £8.75 million between 2007 and 2010, ING bank paid $619 million for violating US sanctions in 2012) paid significant charges due to noncompliance (Meral, 2020).

American House Committee on Appropriations in 2014 echoed a similar concern with the concealment of illegal activities by traffickers and terrorist organizations through the use of Bitcoins, other forms of peer-to-peer digital currency used to perform illegal money laundering and illegal funds transfers (Campbell-Verduyn, 2018). Bitcoins provide a sense of anonymity to terrorist and fraudulent users who seek to take advantage of the private nature of the currency that operates as a decentralized transaction (Gladstein, 2021). The fact that Bitcoin can be used as an international payment system without being transparent with the user's identity make it a difficult challenge for international authorities to prevent or monitor the use of this currency to fund terrorist activities (Gladstein, 2021). Bitcoin cannot be stopped by authorities, and transacting with trusted third parties is not a requirement; instead, unknown parties download software from internet and send money anonymously within minutes to various individuals without interaction or permission from the government (Gladstein, 2021). The individual's use of the bitcoin does not contain information (phone number, email address, identifying information) that is traceable to the individual identity of location where the individual resides or who the individuals will be going to (Gladstein, 2021). The second report issued by the FATF in 2015 addressed the need for cryptocurrency to be implicated in terrorist financing as evidence by the American teenager who pled guilty to promoting cryptocurrency efforts as a means of funding the Islamic State (Campbell-Verduyn, 2018). Money laundering and terrorist funding high-risk levels are intensified through the use of crypto-currency; some banks' risk mitigation efforts to lower the risk posed by crypto-currency are through the use of blockchain technology which creates a unified system which makes it difficult for fraudulent users to operate anonymously (Kerimov et al., 2020). Blockchain allows the banks to use the unified system in which it operates to combat the laundering of funds illegally (Kerimov et al., 2020). Regulators believe the risk of having individuals identify unknown in a cryptocurrency transaction is counteracted by blockchain through the features of this technology; regulators proposed appropriate rules around pseudonymity where users must be identified and personal users' data are made available to the regulators (Kerimov et al., 2020).

Another tool terrorist use to transfer funds illegally why maintaining anonymity is through use of Limited Liability Corporation (LLC) established in the USA. Bieler (2022) mentioned the United States open more than two million corporations and limited liability companies (LLCs) each year in states that failed to obtain the identity of the owner's information due to their laxed laws; these unknown individuals are beneficial owners who either own or control the entity. This loophole of anonymity provided by the LLC facilitates illegal activities (tax evasion, bribery, money laundering, terrorism financing) to go through the system without detection by the government and regulators (Bieler, 2022). The use of LLCs is a preferred method that global terrorist groups around the world rely on as the best way for them to move their money around the world (Bieler, 2022). There are suggestions to have the public and citizens in general involve in the identification and mitigation of money laundering and terrorist activity funding. The use of a public beneficial ownership database may be helpful in the fight against terrorist funding, money laundering, providing the public access to the information for their review and scrutiny (Bieler, 2022). The governments will allow members of the public and nonprofit organizations (NPOs) to have access to AML and anti-terrorism efforts data for review; this allows the public to scrutinize the information/data which affords some level of transparency and build public trust (Bieler, 2022). This will help bolster public confidence and trust levels in the banking and financial system; this allows the trust to be active stakeholders in finding discrepancies that could lead to bad actors and contrib-uting to the improvement of the quality of the data (Bieler, 2022).

Ehi (2021) pointed out that terrorist actors have recruited money mules to take part in money laundering and terrorist financing activities. Money mules are individuals mule recruited by a criminal to transfers illegally acquired money on behalf of and the direction of that law breaker; these criminals hire mules to move money electronically through bank accounts illegally and assist or move physical currency through various activities and methods (Ehi, 2021). These terrorist actors train and coach the money mules on measures and actions to take to avoid detection by financial institutions and law enforcement authorities (Ehi, 2021). There are suggestions from stakeholders that there could be negative backlash from prohibition on the local and global level of money laundering and terrorist finance risks which end up driving the lawbreakers to go underground; these illegal actors would resolve to continue to operate underground and bypass without AML/combating the financing of terrorism (CFT) controls and government oversight (Campbell-Verduyn, 2018). Banks are a significant stakeholder in the prevention of the financing of terrorism and are required to liaison with law enforcement authorities in the prevention of terrorist activities financing (Mugarura, 2015). Banks who failed to prevent these terrorist financing activities are referred to as villains and punished with penalties for not doing enough to prevent crimes (Mugarura, 2015). For example, ING Bank was fined $619 million by the US government for violation of US sanctions against Cuba, Iran, and other US sanctioned countries (Mugarura, 2015). ING allegedly transported $1.6 billion illegally through banks in the United States by concealing the nature of the activity in 2007; additionally, ING eliminated payment data that would make the transactions transparent and would make available the identity of the sanctioned countries and entities that are parties to the activities (Mugarura, 2015).

The bank accused of assisting clients on how to evade computer filters that are prevention measures that would stop sanctioned entities from gaining access to the US banking system and used shell companies to provide US finance services to sanctioned entities (Mugarura, 2015). ING Bank paid $619 million for violating US sanctions in 2012 (Meral, 2020). There are other banks found to be in violation of US sanctions with areas such as Cuba, Libya, Sudan, and Iran. Credit Suisse paid $536 million to settle charges of illegal transactions involving Iran, Cuba, and Libya in 2009 (Mugarura, 2015). That same year of 2009 Lloyd Bank TSB paid $ 350 million to settle charges relating to the alteration client records relating to Iran, Sudan, and other sanctioned countries; the following year, Barclays Bank settled charges of £298 million for violation of US sanctioned countries and entities rules in 2010 (Mugarura, 2015). Several other banks were punished for violation of US sanction rules. One being Barclays Bank Pic paid $298 million in 2010 for violations of several sanctioned countries' (Iran, North Korea, Myanmar, Sudan) rules enforced by the United States; then in 2016, Barclays banks had to pay $2.5 million for violations of Zimbabwe sanctions (Meral, 2020). The public awareness to the severity of sanctions violations when in 2012 HSBC bank had to pay $1.92 billion dollars to state authorities illegal transferring money into the USA (Meral, 2020).

There are civil lawsuits brought by local citizens who were identified as victims of terrorist attacks against banks (Mugarura, 2015). These civil actions claimed that banks facilitate terrorist activities and were reckless in their failure to use KYC procedures to monitor wire transfer constituting to them suffering harm which makes the banks liable (Mugarura, 2015). Some of the sued banks were Credit Lyonnais, UBS, Nat West, Bank of China (BOC), American Express Bank, and Lebanese Canadian Bank (formerly, a division of Royal Bank of Canada) filed by an Israeli organization called Shurat HaD (Mugarura, 2015). In one of the lawsuit 50 Israeli citizens injured and some with or who had relatives killed in Hamas rocket attacks sought damages of $750 million; the claim made was BOC should have known about the customer and their wire transfers based on Customer Due Diligence (CDD) and account monitoring activities (Mugarura, 2015). BOC was accused of failing to use prudent judgment on monitoring of account activity, identifying red flags such as cash over $100,000 withdrawn the same day they arrived (Mugarura, 2015). The US government place emphasis on the rules requiring banks to have effective KYC procedures to avoid the risk of violation of sanctions. For example, sanctions compliance can be met through the use of the SWIFT system along with the use of application such as KYC Registry that provides information about the customers in international trade/cross borders (Meral, 2020).

Banks are not the only institutions that have to abide by laws relating to sanctioned areas; the government has extended these requirements to NPO that operates in the sanctioned region and provides humanitarian aid to those regions. Eckert (2021) stated the restrictions placed on NPO relating to sanctions require greater understanding between NPOs, financial institutions, and the government that will bring improvement to the regulatory and policy environment. This understanding among these respective stakeholders will assist in the development of tools to facilitate information-sharing (Eckert, 2021). The use of assigned and designated work streams were used to develop standardized lists of information that banks utilized to conduct due diligence on NPO customers, make available clarify of regulatory requirements and risk guidance, carried out through the revision of the BSA/AML Examination Manual to implement FATF Recommendation and solutions to at risk NPO transfers (Eckert, 2021). The use of KYC registry and SWIFT system affords transparency in the transactions shared information; the US Senate stated the significant and material nature of financial crimes and laundering in the United States to the tune of US$ 500 billion to US$ 1 trillion criminal income are laundered (Meral, 2020). The SWIFT system can be utilized to perform sanctions screening online through its online screening service for incoming and outgoing messages of various nature while cross checking against Office of Foreign Assets Control (OFAC) and European Union with sanctions lists (Meral, 2020). Sanctions laws have negatively impacted humanitarian to individuals who rely on this aid survival.

The negative impact on humanitarian aid has been an ongoing issue. The US sanctions had a devastated impact along with the imposed counterterrorism (CT) measures on humanitarian action (Eckert, 2021). Many groups that provide humanitarian assistance to countries listed on the US sanctions list (Syria, Iraq, Yemen, Somalia, Nigeria, Pakistan, Afghanistan) faced roadblocks and were unable to deliver humanitarian aid (Eckert, 2021). Eckert (2021) mentioned there have been concerns about the impact of sanctions on humanitarian action which has been recognized as a pressing problem by the United Nations which affects the delivery of humanitarian aid. The impact of sanctions on humanitarian aid to Iraq has caused global outcry to the controversy surrounding the humanitarian consequences of these sanctions (Eckert, 2021). This has received attention from the United Nations who recommends the transformational shift away from comprehensive sanctions and pivot to the used of more targeted measures (Eckert, 2021). The UN awareness was heightened to the sanction impacts on innocent Iraqis and children in the hundreds of thousands who died as a result of imposed sanctions (Eckert, 2021). There was a pivot from sanctions that are broad economic sanctions which caused disproportional harm to the use of smart targeted sanctions geared to the actual decision-makers who violated the international norms and their main supporters (Eckert, 2021). However, there are some nations on the sanctions list that receive some sort of limited exemption due to humanitarian needs. Eckert (2021) pointed to humanitarian exception to UN sanctions on Somalia first rolled out in 2010 as a result of devastating needs famine as a result of environmental disasters (floods, cyclones, unprecedented desert locust swarms) resulting in rising conflict in the region. Somalia exemption was eventually cancelled due to lack of humanitarian groups being able to operate in areas controlled by the Islamic terrorist group Al-Shabaab (Eckert, 2021).

# Chapter 10

# Office of Foreign Assets Control (OFAC) Compliance Practices

The Office of Foreign Assets Control (OFAC) implements and manages US economic sanctions. OFAC was established in 1950 by US Treasury and was originally called Office of Foreign Funds Control (FFC) with the objective of preventing Nazis in 1940 from using occupied countries' belongings (Meral, 2020). OFAC maintains a website where it publishes a list as noted by Meral (2020) which entails countries, companies, and individuals who act on behalf of terrorist that are placed on a blocked person list known as a Specially Designated Nationals (SDNs) Blocked Persons List. Countries that are on a blocked list are prohibited from sending funds to and from the United States; for example, individuals holding bank account in Nigeria are blocked from sending or receiving funds to the United States and United Kingdom (Ehi, 2021). OFAC list is a government-made list of SDNs who perceived to threaten America's national security (Altabet, 2022). Seelke (2020) mentioned property and interests of individuals on SDN list subjected to US jurisdiction are blocked; US citizens and companies are prohibited from engaging in transactions with companies on the restricted list. The failure of an organization to effectively screen/assess new customers against the SDN list of prohibited entities, countries, and individuals can expose them to potential lawsuits. The TransUnion Company was exposed to a lawsuit brought by a class of plaintiffs who sued the credit reporting organization on the grounds that the firm had failed to use reasonable procedures to validate credit files accuracy (Altabet, 2022). It was noted that there were inaccuracies on plaintiffs listed in TransUnion's files as potentially on SDN because the company fall short of performing due diligence that credits files to the OFAC list (Altabet, 2022). Individuals with the same first and last name as an individual on the OFAC list was identified as a potential match to the terrorist database by TransUnion which generated many false positives (Altabet, 2022).

Banks are required to implement the SDN and block list as part of their control environment to ensure activities and transaction should not be executed with these individuals. This is possible through the implementation of risk screening and risk profile for new accounts being established at the bank. A form

Compliance and Financial Crime Risk in Banks, 107–111
Copyright © 2024 Sophia Beckett Velez
Published under exclusive licence by Emerald Publishing Limited
doi:10.1108/978-1-83549-041-920241010

of screening is the risk profile screening where the three lines of defense are engaged in the process of identifying and preventing possible fraud (Rathod, 2022). The three lines of defense in the bank involve risk-averse individuals (first line of defense bank operation unit risk owner, risk review team second line of defense, third line of defense chief anti-money laundering [AML] compliance officer responsible for complete control) who monitor anticipated high-risk events such as transactions in breach of SDN list (Rathod, 2022). For accounts that were established at banks that were listed on the block list, the United States seized those assets. The blocking of assets was highlighted in OFAC-published guidance on explicit issues aligned to the sanction programs such as Venezuela sanctions; US citizens found dealing with individuals, companies, or countries on the SDN list assets were blocked (Venezuela, 2020). Although OFAC operates out of the United States, it based on the UN sanctions application framework (Meral, 2020). The end of the Cold War echoed in the age of the UN sanctions in 1992 that span 7 years of levying sanctions on countries that experienced high levels of armed violence; the motives of these sanctions are to mitigate significant violence, foster peace, reconciliation processes, protect human rights in various parts of Africa plagued with unrests and conflicts (Somalia, Liberia, Angola, Rwanda, Sudan, and Sierra Leone) (Eckert, 2021). There were other conflicted regions namely Libya and Sudan plagued by terrorism that these sanctions were subjected to implement democracy in the Haitian government (Eckert, 2021). The prior president Barack Obama Administration imposed targeted sanctions on Venezuela because of their history and stance on human rights abuses, corruption, and antidemocratic actions; additionally, Trump Administration made significant expansion of economic sanctions in response to increased power of President Nicolás Maduro (Seelke, 2020).

The best way to ensure banks are in compliance with the SDN list is to have proper screening of clients during the onboarding process when they open an account and during the processing of their transactions. Rathod (2022) mentioned OFAC compliance requirements such as the SDN list is compromised when there is improper screening of payment that end up going to a sanctioned entity. There are significant penalties for US companies and individuals found in violation of transacting with countries and people on the SDN list. This website is accessible to the public and is updated frequently with additions and deletions to the list. The SDN list covers terrorists and narcotics smugglers that US citizens are prevented from transacting with as noted in the Trade with the Enemy Act (TWEA) Law (Meral, 2020). Many of the countries on the SDN list and TWEA include countries like Cuba, Iran, Libya Venezuela, and Sudan (Rathod, 2022). The SDN list maintained by OFAC includes individuals and entities selected by Venezuela sanctions authorities and companies under the ownership/controlled by Venezuelans (Venezuela, 2020). Venezuela sanctions program seeks to prevent the legitimacy of the former government known as the Maduro Regime revenue streams; individuals were held accountable who tried to prevent democracy in the country (Venezuela, 2020). US visa were revoked for more than 1,000 Venezuelans and members of their families to crush the Maduro power and its party which controls a de facto National Assembly seated January 5, 2021 (Seelke, 2020).

The current US President Biden Administration was asked by analyst to consider maintaining all sanctions to pressure Maduro into negotiations with the opposing party; on the other hand, individuals suggested removal of broad sanctions that hurt the Venezuelan people without pressuring Maduro's departure while utilizing a targeted/focuse-based sanction implemented with US allies' participation (Seelke, 2020). US Treasury has imposed sanctions on over 150 prominent Venezuelans, foreign individuals' Venezuelan government, and numerous Venezuelan visas were revoked from entering the United States by the Department of State (Venezuela, 2020). US restrictions on prominent Venezuelan individuals (President Maduro, his wife, Cecilia Flores and son, Nicolás Maduro Guerra; Executive, Delcy Rodriguez, Diosdado Cabello, eight supreme court judges, Venezuela army leader, national guard, and national police, governors, director of the central bank, foreign minister) began in 2006; individuals were placed on a block person's list and their properties and prevention of commercial arms sales transactions (Seelke, 2020). US sanctions were imposed on the Venezuelan government, central bank, and state oil company Petróleos de Venezuela, S.A. (PdVSA) (Venezuela, 2020). The US Secretary of State's annual review of Venezuela compliance found the country not complying with US anti-terrorism efforts pursuant to Section 40A of the Arms Export Control Act (22 U.S.C. 2781) which was a most recent violation of May 2020 (Seelke, 2020). The United States prohibited commercial arms sales and retransfers to Venezuela since 2006 (Venezuela, 2020). These Venezuela sanctions were executed while allowing the humanitarian (aid, goods, services) to flow into the country for the people (Venezuela, 2020).The impact of the US sanctions on Venezuelan crude oil had been limited and not as impactful as they might have wanted them to be. The limited impact of sanction on the oil industry in Venezuela has likely had a limited impact, if any, on the US oil industry. Despite an overall lower supply of oil in the US market from the loss of Venezuelan crude oil, the retail gasoline prices in the United States were not exposed to significant increases (Venezuela, 2020).

The Treasury Department's OFAC places restrictions on US citizens' remittances to Cuba and prohibits traveling to Cuba; the United States isolated Cuba partly because of its communist government in the 1960s and placed restrictions through the Cuban Assets Control Regulations (CACR) (Sullivan, 2018). The Treasury Department's OFAC places restrictions on US citizens sending funds to Cuba and prohibits them from traveling to Cuba; the United States isolated Cuba partly because of its communist government in the 1960s and placed restrictions through the CACR (Sullivan, 2018). In more recent times, the US President Barack Obama came to power in 2008 and decided to relax some of the restrictions prior US presidents placed in Cuba. Erisman (2021) mentioned Obama policy gestures, re-established formal diplomatic relations with Cuba, use of Executive Powers to ease US citizens visit to the island, Cuban Americans were now able to send remittances to their relatives in Cuba, Havana removed from the SDN list, toward Cuba was dramatic and draw media attention. Sullivan (2018) mentioned Obama Administration lifted restrictions in stages as follows: 2009 family travel and remittances, 2011 other types of travel restrictions lifted (religious, educational, people-to-people exchanges), any US person can send remittances to Cuba, the year 2014 moved away from a sanctions-based policy toward an engagement one. Similarly, Erisman (2021) stated Obama Administration in 2014 allowed Cuba private sector businesses such as products of privately run/cooperative farms that are not state owned/operated to export/sell their Cuban products to the United States. This was a major boost in Cuba's private sector and country's economy (Erisman, 2021). OFAC followed suit in 2015 and 2016 by amending the embargo regulations up to five times to carry out the new policy; OFAC initially authorized 12 categories of travel, eliminated limits of travel per diems, increased nonfamily remittances amounts, and allowed various types of remittances (Sullivan, 2018).

The increase in dollar amounts in 2015 by OFAC that US citizens sending funds to Cuba or taking funds in the country were as follows: remittances to a Cuban national limit $2,000 per quarter, carry up to $10,000 in remittances to Cuba (Sullivan, 2018). Thereafter, OFAC made further changes to their regulations and removed the dollar limits on nonfamily remittances/donative remittances to Cuban nationals, as well as they removed limits on amounts licensed travelers can bring into Cuba (Sullivan, 2018). There were changes made in 2016 by the departments of Treasury and Commerce that improved relations between the United States and Cuba relating to the health sector. Erisman (2021) referred to the major health sector changes as three different types as follows: (1) US jurisdiction can engage in all transactions relating to joint medical research projects with Cubans; (2) US jurisdiction are able to engage in transactions after obtaining approval from US Food and Drug Administration (FDA) of Cuban-origin pharmaceuticals for various stages (discovery and development, preclinical research, clinical research, regulatory review, regulatory approval and licensing, regulatory postmarket activities, importation into the United States); (3) all to market, sell, distribute in United States. Additionally, OFAC removed dollar limits for donating funds to Cubans, allowed people-to-people educational travel for individuals, allowed importation of Cuban products (alcohol, tobacco) without limitations (Sullivan, 2018). President Trump passed actions in August 2019 to block and freeze the property and interests of the Maduro government in the United States; the United States prohibit the persons from engaging in transactions with the Maduro government without special permission/exception per OFAC E.O. 13884. The restrictions apply to non-US persons that assist or support the Maduro government, including foreign energy companies transacting with PdVSA; the E.O. 13884 sanctioned five individuals and several vessels and aircraft (Erisman, 2021). Accommodations were made to allow assistance to the Venezuelan people where OFAC issued licenses to permit the delivery of food, agricultural commodities, and medicine, remittances, international organizations, and communications services (Erisman, 2021). OFAC in 2020 issued guidance asking nonprofit organization (NPO) delivering humanitarian aid to Venezuela to report sanctions-related barriers they encounter so they can have a resolution (Erisman, 2021).

There are some sanctions reintroduced after the election of the subsequent president Donald Trump. The Trump Presidency in 2017 rollbacks US interactions with Cuba which eliminated individual people-to-people travel and financial transactions with companies in Cuba (Sullivan, 2018). Erisman (2021) stated the Trump Administration kept some of Obama's reforms by continuing diplomatic recognition, but there was a reversion to a hard-line stance that was maintained prior to Obama administration. The reversion to a hard-line against Cuba was carried out by lowering the number of staff at the US embassy; this impacted the caring out of routine business to minimal levels (Erisman, 2021). There were restrictions reintroduced to traveling to the island, and remittances to Cuba from the United States were tightened, importation of oil to Havana was disrupted, which spawned another energy crisis for the country (Erisman, 2021). US sanctions regulatory agency OFAC adopted a policy in 2014 recognizing the inherent risks in conflict areas where humanitarian agents operate subjecting them to that humanitarian assistance end up in the hands of terrorist organizations (Rathod, 2022). Softening the blow of sanctions on humanitarian aid and the well-being of the local citizens in need has been at the forefront of the United States and United Nations. There are three significant challenges humanitarian groups face as noted by Eckert (2021) namely: (1) lack of adequate legal protection and clarity for agents acting in sanction regions; (2) NPOs face with limitations to transfer funds to high-risk regions due to over-compliance or fear of regulatory scrutiny; (3) humanitarian funders off load risk to NPOs and beneficiaries noted in written contracts. During the 1990s, the United Nations imposed targeted sanctions on listed individuals and companies whose assets were frozen with limited access by way of an exemption (Eckert, 2021).These exemptions were granted for specific expenses (rent, food, medicine, travel for judicial proceedings, religious travel) which was adopted for several regions (Democratic Republic of the Congo [DRC], Sudan, Libya, Guinea-Bissau, Central African Republic [CAR], Mali, Yemen, South Sudan) sanctions committees (Eckert, 2021). Sullivan (2018) asserts Cuban Assets Control Regulations (CACR) amendment in 2015 allowed Cuban and related NGOs to operate without the burden of certain remittance limitations on human projects, allowed activities of known human rights entities, support institutions aligned to fostering transition to peaceful democracy, companies that strengthen civil society, encouraging growth of small and private firms. Venezuela (2020) highlights the United States actively assisting the US Agency for International Development (USAID) with effort to reduce humanitarian crisis under Venezuela Regional Crisis Response which includes humanitarian programming for individuals (migrants, refugees, host communities, vulnerable Venezuelans) inside Venezuela. USAID efforts as it relates to (water, sanitation, hygiene health, food, protection support services) are made available in Venezuela and in neighboring countries (Brazil, Colombia, Ecuador, Peru) and receive support from the United States (Venezuela, 2020). USAID in 2020 contributed over $563 million in US funding for the Venezuela Regional Crisis Response as of 2017 (Venezuela, 2020).

# Chapter 11

# Capital Requirements – Effective Practices

The continuous global economic turmoil and significant unanticipated losses in mega banks have shed light on the ineffective delivery of capital regulation (Tanda, 2015; Yeoh, 2016). There has been limited research on effective capital regulation measure to address these significant losses (Berger et al., 2018; Dowd & Hutchinson, 2016). And now more than ever, banks are faced with insolvency leading to bank runs. Despite this factor, there is a lack of clear information and guidance for effective application of the regulator's requirement for capital compliance, banks still have to strive toward meeting and demonstrating compliance with the requirements of Basel III, Dodd–Frank Bill 2010, and other regulations passed after 2008 recession. Banks that failed to demonstrate compliance with these costly and time-consuming compliance requirements are often penalized. Global banks found to be in noncompliance with regulatory compliance measures were dealt harshly by the regulators. There were consensus statements that had six or more votes from the 10 banking finance experts across the United States who participated in the qualitative e-Delphi study on how to recognize a senior manager's effective practice toward capital regulation in large banks. These statements related to compliance activities such as: maintenance of effective and independent compliance consistent with the organizational objectives, clear definition of data source for compliance analytics, ensure compliance monitoring and reporting activities promptly to upper management, top leadership must be a champion of code of ethics, strong morals and integrity, right products for clients, understanding regulatory compliance.

Regulators believe that their guidelines geared at sensitivity to risk and the rules they roll out will equip banks to effectively achieve objectives of a safe and sound banking environment (Hogan, 2021). Stress testing required by the regulators to run as part of the capital calculations and filings have been deemed counterproductive to meeting banking objectives. Herring (2016) noted stress testing has been identified as a useful compliance activity, but bank managers have complained about its complex, onerous nature that pull them from mission-critical business objectives (Herring, 2016). Loh (2021) discussed the struggles bankers face brought about their legal obligation to report suspicious and fraudulent activities conducted by the clients they provide services. This

Compliance and Financial Crime Risk in Banks, 113–124
Copyright © 2024 Sophia Beckett Velez
Published under exclusive licence by Emerald Publishing Limited
doi:10.1108/978-1-83549-041-920241011

conflict of interest role as agents to report fraudulent activities to the government while striving to maximize profits and provide service to customer has been a tug-of-war for bankers; the lax of regulation and enforcement with the growing money laundering scandals often displays the banks' role in leaving the gate wide-opened while they are expected to be gatekeepers incentivized by the need to make a profit (Loh, 2021). It has been noted that bank managements are ready to take reputation and regulatory risks if it garners them a financial return (Loh, 2021). It is important, as noted by the panelist to find the balance between meeting regulators' objectives while still meeting the organizational objectives. Bezzina et al. (2014) highlighted the importance of banks having defined goals, identifying risks and vulnerabilities the company face as an essential factor in meeting their objectives. Banks being aware of their risks and vulnerabilities are effective tools in identifying and managing risks. Duncan (2021) mentioned the enterprise-wide risk assessment (EWRA) program as a means to manage risk while identifying issues threatening the institution's objectives. This could be a good hybrid model of meeting both the regulatory and the organizational objectives. The consensus voting on the various statements that met the 6 or greater out of 10 votes are displayed in Tables 11.1–11.7 (Velez, 2020).

Duncan (2021) states the bank should consider changing and emerging requirements within the financial environment as well as focusing on meeting stakeholder value. This entails taking into consideration risk impacts internal and external against mitigation strategies; the results from the EWRA assessments would be utilized into strategic initiatives to achieve the objectives (Duncan, 2021). The EWRA methodology highlights the importance of senior management and Board of Directors in the framework of the company's risk environment by establishing risk policies, understanding the risks and impact on the business, designing a risk management program, monitoring employees application of using effective controls, and increase awareness and management of risks (Duncan, 2021). The importance of the Board of Directors in the establishment of policies and procedures, controls, compliance, appropriate incentive, organizational structure in setting the tone at the top of company effective risk management program (Goldberg, 2017). Ghosh (2021) asserts Board of Directors need to be involved with the periodic reviews of the compliance systems and procedures within the bank to have effective compliance function. Eastburn and Sharland (2017) highlight the importance of a respectable risk culture that can mitigate the growing risk banks face through ensuring managerial decisions are part of the framework of this risk culture. Board of Directors' active role in informing decision management makes through established governance policies can help to mitigate the growing risk banks face. The financial risk banks face from business activities undertaken by management by ensuring prespecified tolerances and limits are established that informs our decisions; it is important that leaders lead by example (Eastburn & Sharland, 2017). The considerations allude to having a pre-established framework of prespecified tolerances for employees to follow and leaders leading by examples through putting these initiatives into practice can improve the risk culture within the bank. Gatzert and Schmit (2016) mention an effective risk culture can inform managers ethical awareness effected through their choices and reduction of fraudulent behavior.

Table 11.1. Compliance Practices on Organizational Objectives 3rd Round Data: Consensus.

| Statement | Ratings | Total Number of Panelist Who Selected Each Ratings |
|---|---|---|
| Statement 58 – Compliance practices toward capital regulation that can be effective in reducing losses incudes maintenance of effective and independent compliance consistent with the organizational objectives. | | |
| | Highly undesirable: Will have major negative effect. | 0 |
| | Undesirable: Will have a negative effect with little or no positive effect. | 0 |
| | Neither desirable nor undesirable: Will have equal positive and negative effects. | 2 |
| | Desirable: Will have a positive effect with minimum negative effects. | 4 |
| | Highly desirable: Will have a positive effect and little or no negative effect. | 6 |
| | Definitely infeasible: Cannot be implemented (unworkable). | 0 |
| | Probably infeasible: Some indication this cannot be implemented. | 0 |
| | May or may not be feasible: Contradictory | 1 |

*(Continued)*

Table 11.1. *(Continued)*

| Statement | Ratings | Total Number of Panelist Who Selected Each Ratings |
|---|---|---|
| | evidence this can be implemented. | |
| | Probably feasible: Some indication this can be implemented. | 1 |
| | Definitely feasible: Can be implemented. | 6 |

Table 11.2. Compliance Practices on Clear Definition of Data Sources 3rd Round Data: Consensus.

| Statement | Ratings | Total Number of Panelist Who Selected Each Ratings |
|---|---|---|
| Statement 65 – Compliance practices toward capital regulation that can be effective in reducing losses includes clear definition of data source for compliance analytics. | | |
| | Highly undesirable: Will have major negative effect. | 0 |
| | Undesirable: Will have a negative effect with little or no positive effect. | 1 |
| | Neither desirable nor undesirable: Will have equal positive and negative effects. | 0 |

Table 11.2. *(Continued)*

| Statement | Ratings | Total Number of Panelist Who Selected Each Ratings |
|---|---|---|
| | Desirable: Will have a positive effect with minimum negative effects. | 2 |
| | Highly desirable: Will have a positive effect and little or no negative effect. | 6 |
| | Definitely infeasible: Cannot be implemented (unworkable). | 1 |
| | Probably infeasible: Some indication this cannot be implemented. | 1 |
| | May or may not be feasible: Contradictory evidence this can be implemented. | 2 |
| | Probably feasible: Some indication this can be implemented. | 3 |
| | Definitely feasible: Can be implemented. | 4 |

Table 11.3. Compliance Practices on Monitoring and Reporting 3rd Round Data: Consensus.

| Statement | Ratings | Total Number of Panelist Who Selected Each Ratings |
|---|---|---|
| Statement 66 – Compliance practices toward capital regulation that can be effective in reducing losses includes monitoring and reporting | | |

*(Continued)*

Table 11.3. *(Continued)*

| Statement | Ratings | Total Number of Panelist Who Selected Each Ratings |
|---|---|---|
| activities promptly to upper management. | | |
| | Highly undesirable: Will have major negative effect. | 0 |
| | Undesirable: Will have a negative effect with little or no positive effect. | 0 |
| | Neither desirable nor undesirable: Will have equal positive and negative effects. | 0 |
| | Desirable: Will have a positive effect with minimum negative effects. | 4 |
| | Highly desirable: Will have a positive effect and little or no negative effect. | 6 |
| | Definitely infeasible: Cannot be implemented (unworkable). | 0 |
| | Probably infeasible: Some indication this cannot be implemented. | 0 |
| | May or may not be feasible: Contradictory evidence this can be implemented. | 0 |
| | Probably feasible: Some indication this can be implemented. | 3 |
| | Definitely feasible: Can be implemented. | 7 |

Table 11.4. Compliance Practices on Code of Ethics 3rd Round Data: Consensus.

| Statement | Ratings | Total Number of Panelist Who Selected Each Ratings |
|---|---|---|
| Statement 78 – Compliance practices toward capital regulation that can be effective in reducing losses includes top leadership must be a champion of code of ethics. | | |
| | Highly undesirable: Will have major negative effect. | 0 |
| | Undesirable: Will have a negative effect with little or no positive effect. | 1 |
| | Neither desirable nor undesirable: Will have equal positive and negative effects. | 1 |
| | Desirable: Will have a positive effect with minimum negative effects. | 2 |
| | (Highly desirable: Will have a positive effect and little or no negative effect. | 7 |
| | Definitely infeasible: Cannot be implemented (unworkable). | 2 |
| | Probably infeasible: Some indication this cannot be implemented. | 0 |
| | May or may not be feasible: Contradictory evidence this can be implemented. | 1 |

*(Continued)*

Table 11.4. *(Continued)*

| Statement | Ratings | Total Number of Panelist Who Selected Each Ratings |
|---|---|---|
| | Probably feasible: Some indication this can be implemented. | 4 |
| | Definitely feasible: Can be implemented. | 3 |

Table 11.5. Compliance Practices on Morals and Integrity 3rd Round Data: Consensus.

| Statement | Ratings | Total Number of Panelist Who Selected Each Ratings |
|---|---|---|
| Statement 89 – Compliance practices toward capital regulation that can be effective in reducing losses includes strong morals and integrity. | | |
| | Highly undesirable: Will have major negative effect. | 0 |
| | Undesirable: Will have a negative effect with little or no positive effect. | 0 |
| | Neither desirable nor undesirable: Will have equal positive and negative effects. | 1 |
| | Desirable: Will have a positive effect with minimum negative effects. | 3 |

Table 11.5. *(Continued)*

| Statement | Ratings | Total Number of Panelist Who Selected Each Ratings |
|---|---|---|
| | Highly desirable: Will have a positive effect and little or no negative effect. | 6 |
| | Definitely infeasible: Cannot be implemented (unworkable). | 1 |
| | Probably infeasible: Some indication this cannot be implemented. | 2 |
| | May or may not be feasible: Contradictory evidence this can be implemented. | 4 |

Table 11.6. Compliance Practices on Right Product 3rd Round Data: Consensus.

| Statement | Ratings | Total Number of Panelist Who Selected Each Ratings |
|---|---|---|
| Statement 90 – Compliance practices toward capital regulation that can be effective in reducing losses includes right products for clients. | | |
| | Highly undesirable: Will have major negative effect. | 0 |
| | Undesirable: Will have a negative effect with little or no positive effect. | 0 |

*(Continued)*

Table 11.6. *(Continued)*

| Statement | Ratings | Total Number of Panelist Who Selected Each Ratings |
|---|---|---|
| | Neither desirable nor undesirable: Will have equal positive and negative effects. | 1 |
| | Desirable: Will have a positive effect with minimum negative effects. | 5 |
| | Highly desirable: Will have a positive effect and little or no negative effect. | 6 |
| | Definitely infeasible: Cannot be implemented (unworkable). | 0 |
| | Probably infeasible: Some indication this cannot be implemented. | 1 |
| | May or may not be feasible: Contradictory evidence this can be implemented. | 2 |
| | Probably feasible: Some indication this can be implemented. | 4 |
| | Definitely feasible: Can be implemented. | 1 |

Table 11.7. Compliance Practices on Understanding Regulatory Compliance 3rd Round Data: Consensus.

| Statement | Ratings | Total Number of Panelist Who Selected Each Ratings |
|---|---|---|
| Statement 91 – Compliance practices toward capital regulation that can be effective in reducing losses includes understanding regulatory compliance. | | |
| | Highly undesirable: Will have major negative effect. | 0 |
| | Undesirable: Will have a negative effect with little or no positive effect. | 0 |
| | Neither desirable nor undesirable: Will have equal positive and negative effects. | 1 |
| | Desirable: Will have a positive effect with minimum negative effects. | 6 |
| | Highly desirable: Will have a positive effect and little or no negative effect. | 5 |
| | Definitely infeasible: Cannot be implemented (unworkable). | 0 |
| | Probably infeasible: Some indication this cannot be implemented. | 0 |
| | May or may not be feasible: Contradictory evidence this can be implemented. | 3 |

*(Continued)*

Table 11.7. *(Continued)*

| Statement | Ratings | Total Number of Panelist Who Selected Each Ratings |
|---|---|---|
| | Probably feasible: Some indication this can be implemented. | 3 |
| | Definitely feasible: Can be implemented. | 2 |

# Chapter 12

# Bank Secrecy Act Anti-Money Laundering Compliance Practices – Effective Practices

There are Bank Secrecy Act (BSA) anti-money laundering (AML) practices when implemented within a framework that includes executive management at the governance and board levels can garner success in the banking sector. The panel of experts met consensus on the role of top leadership having an effective compliance practice; the panelist vote on the statement "top leadership must be a champion of code of ethics," which met the six out of 10 votes needed for consensus (Velez, 2020). The role of top leadership is highlighted by ElYacoubi (2020) as an important foundation in a sound risk and compliance culture which starts at the top in banks. The Basel Committee on Banking Supervision (BCBS), US and UK regulators and other international regulatory bodies noted having a financial stability board whose role entails monitoring activities, recommendations regarding the global financial system, positioning the right leadership at the Board level, are just as important as having the right culture within the banking organization (ElYacoubi, 2020). This highlights the importance of a top-down approach where top senior management are stakeholders of the risk culture, have a long-term risk view, and hold individuals accountable (ElYacoubi, 2020). The tone at the top is significantly important and plays a key role in the nurturing of business ethics and morals (ElYacoubi, 2020). Top leadership who sets the tone at the top is a part of the first line of the defense that creates or influences the creation of the company's policies and procedures, mold the risk culture of the organization. The policies and procedures of the bank discusses that how and what management and it's employees of the bank should carry out the various business activities of the firm. This covers the control activities, approvals, and review processes management should execute when conducting the bank's business. These policies and procedures impact the nature/temperature of the control environment which can range from weak to strong. The tone at the top establishes the temperature of how these procedures and policies will be received by the employee, whether taken seriously or laxed on how they view them. Helena and Madsen (2021) stressed the importance of having the right tone at which they established the ethical atmosphere in the workplace by leaders of the

Compliance and Financial Crime Risk in Banks, 125–142

Copyright © 2024 Sophia Beckett Velez

Published under exclusive licence by Emerald Publishing Limited

doi:10.1108/978-1-83549-041-920241012

organization. This tone set by management trickles – down to the firm's employees; managers who set a tone that upholds ethical values will impact the employees becoming involved in upholding ethical values within the firm (Helena & Madsen, 2021).

Banks as an organization either have a compliance environment that is either passive or active. It should be noted that a positive and active compliance environment is one that has proactive responsiveness, put into action a set of rules and standards, open to change without disruption of its daily system's structure and functions (Helena & Madsen, 2021). This active approach has all hands-on board working in concert for the well-being of the corporation and its stakeholders in a proactive compliance environment (Helena & Madsen, 2021). This inclusive approach will take all lines of defense within the bank working together to achieve the company's compliance objectives. Ghosh (2021) mentioned having the various lines of defenses involved in the monitoring of the compliance environment in the bank which includes: (i) First line of defense who are business level executives/managing directors (create policies and procedures, personnel communication), (ii) Second line of defense Chief Risk Officer (monitoring of AML/combating the financing of terrorism policies) independent of business line responsibilities, (iii) Third line of defense – internal audit (audit banks activities and report to audit committee). These three lines of defense work collectively to create a low risk compliance environment based on controls and monitoring activities or it could be the opposite that contributes to a high risk compliance environment due to their lack of participation in the monitoring of the environment. Rifai and Tisnanta (2022) noted banks are required as part of their BSA AML framework to implement various teams (cybersecurity, fraud prevention units, BSA/AML management boards, AML intelligence units, AML analysts/investigators, risk departments, trained network administrators) who should work collectively to foster an effective compliance environment. A part of this effort of an effective compliance environment is to have an enterprise-wide risk assessment (EWRA) completed to ensure potential risks to the bank's environment are identified and addressed/mitigated.

The EWRA methodology which identifies potential risks faced by the firm should be approved by the Board of Directors; this adds credibility and minimized biases in assessment results (Duncan, 2021). The EWRA methodology with the Board's approval communicates purpose and direction of the bank, sets the risk appetite, which influences the tolerable risk the bank can undertake, measurement approach, and risk treatments within and outside the tolerable limits (Duncan, 2021). The panel of experts mentioned in one of the consensus statements that banks need to understand regulatory compliance which can contribute to an effective strategy (Velez, 2020). Banks need to have a good understanding of regulatory compliance, the published requirements, and apply those to their significant risk exposure. ElYacoubi (2020) discusses risk-based approach (RBA) that entails various bodies/stakeholders (countries, competent authorities, banks) understanding risks exposure in various areas (money laundering, terrorism financing) and apply mitigating measures to the aligned level of risk. RBA is a quantitative methodology used to understand the significant risk and apply mitigating measures that will probably reduce risk, not necessarily eliminate risk all together (ElYacoubi, 2020). Bank management would calculate materiality and apply this materiality to the business line item/segment to determine areas that are significant to the business quantitatively. Then the bank will examine those significant areas and map them to risk exposure identified (fraud, terrorist funding, money laundering) and identify mitigating compliance controls. ElYacoubi (2020) asserts banks would need to perform an identification of risk factors, classifications, and scorings; these scorings should provide some transparency into whether these areas are high, medium, or low risk. Risk associated to AML/CFT will entail management judgment as there are no universally agreed upon and accepted methodology supported by governments or the banking sector that stipulated the nature of RBA (ElYacoubi, 2020). On the other hand, there is a consensus of opinion variations of risk within each country, organization, and situation (ElYacoubi, 2020). However, the Board of Directors inform some level of consistency by creating policies that provide governance, mitigation strategies to prevent and manage AML/CFT risk exposure.

The Board's published policy statement, their importance to the organization, and their commitment to maintaining an acceptable risk culture results are examined by external stakeholders (regulators, examiners) in relation to EWRA findings and bank examinations (Duncan, 2021). The Board's motivation and involvement is setting the temperature, for the bank's risk culture is taken into consideration when examiners review the company's compliance environment. The 2020 version of the US BSA/AML Examination Manual emphasized the importance of EWRA results in having a direct impact on the understanding bank examiners have of the bank's risk profile and help in the scaling/scoping used in the planning of audits (Duncan, 2021). Duncan (2021) states senior management should be engaged in the construction of effective risk practices. Loh (2021) mentioned the banking sector environment is plagued with money laundering risks. The EWRA program engages several bank teams and control activities that can be used to effectively raise risk awareness within the bank's environment and risk mitigation measures (Duncan, 2021). The execution of risk mitigation practices can be decentralized to decision-making conducted down, across, and making employees accountable for using effective controls (Duncan, 2021). The Board of Directors have a continuous role and involvement with the intention of safeguarding the company's asset and creating stakeholders value (Duncan, 2021). The implementation of effective risk management entails identification and analysis of money laundering risks (Duncan, 2021). This is a step in the approach of meeting the compliance requirements launched by global regulators.

Banks are investing a significant amount of their budgets on technology that will help them meet regulatory AML compliance obligations while improving the management of their business. ElYacoubi (2020) asserts banks have global AML/CFT regulatory obligations to meet, which requires significant investments in technology to be compliant. This is aligned to the panel of expert's consensus on compliance statement that requires banks to have clear definition of data source for compliance analytics to meet compliance obligations (Velez, 2020). This technology should be able to provide transparency in the nature of the data (who, what, where, how) received, slice and dice the data in a meaningful way so that it makes sense and easy to understand, and afford the ease of submitting the required reporting information to the regulators. Technological advancements/improvements are visible globally in the banking sector investments in heavy upgrades (IT systems, data protection, improve mobile banking, digital customer experiences) within banks (Panda & Joy, 2020). These technological improvements are targeted to address areas (cyber and information security, advanced analytics, big data) of regulatory concerns that expose banks to risks (Panda & Joy, 2020). Global bank spending on IT expenses grew in US dollars from 261.1 billion in 2018 to 296.5 billion in 20214; Bank of America spent USD 16 billion for global technology and operations, JP Morgan Chase spent USD 10.8 billion in 2017 on technology, Citigroup Inc. USD 8 billion (Panda & Joy, 2020). Data management efficiencies gained from the use of RegTech is essential to AML and EWRA competencies. The regulator has successfully implemented cybersecurity framework. Ghosh (2021) mentioned proactive cyber surveillance framework can be used to automate the flow of data from supervised entities; this will add credibility to completeness and accuracy of data quality while minimizing compliance risk in those regulated entities. Lai (2018) mentioned RegTech can be useful to banks in meeting prudential risk management, compliance, and cybersecurity.

RegTech application/automated controls make it possible to automate the AML process and reduce manual intervention and bank risk data aggregation (Lai, 2018). RegTech is an advanced automated digital identity verification and technological innovation that will offer solution in retaining profitable customers in high-risk businesses coupled with continuous client due diligence controls (ElYacoubi, 2020). There are changes made to the digitization of manual reporting and compliance processes through RegTech. Regulatory compliance efficiency and real time reporting enables RegTech, which Meager (2017) asserts this technology helps banks in complying with compliance requirements required by regulatory bodies. RegTech developments should be partnered with automation of significant processes to execute effective cybersecurity in banks (Meager, 2017). There are regulatory guidelines rolled out to help banks address their cybersecurity requirements. Rifai and Tisnanta (2022) continue to say that Financial Crime Enforcement Network (FinCEN) cybersecurity guidelines address how to regulate financial services and the integration of cyber incidents within AML programs. This will include incorporating compliance units in every information management and information security department and all hands-on board from various stakeholders (senior money laundering bank managers, brokerage houses, other financial services) (Rifai & Tisnanta, 2022). It should be noted the importance of training and knowledge sharing as part of the framework to address knowledge areas (company's cybersecurity regimes, resources, security protocols) than can increase the understanding of BSA obligations related to cyber laundering and cyber-related crimes (Rifai & Tisnanta, 2022). The importance of the continuous monitoring of compliance functions includes keeping the Chief Compliance Officer (CCO) in the loop of things through enhanced reporting and overall enhancement of the compliance culture (Ghosh, 2021). The reporting and communication to the stakeholders and CCO can be improved through the use of RegTech. The digitization of reporting and compliance processes through RegTech has enabled a real-time and proportionate regulatory regime to executive management and regulators. RegTech has been referred to as the solution to the significantly increasing compliance costs in an environment that is fast-paced with continuous regulatory changes that require voluminous data reporting and disclosures (ElYacoubi, 2020). RegTech will speed up information availability and response time and allow bank managers their regulatory obligations instantaneously, and in a real time (ElYacoubi, 2020). RegTech enables banks to meet local regulations and global AML/CFT regulatory obligations in a cost-effective manner; the compilation and submission of information is automated, which helps banks to facilitate effective delivery of regulatory obligations (ElYacoubi, 2020). RegTech's strengths lie in its ability to monitor all systems across countries and databases in a holistic instead of relying on snippets of information (ElYacoubi, 2020).

This heightened use of technology by banks and other stakeholders in the financial services industry is highlighted by Meager (2017) as one of the means necessary for financial institutions to comply with regulations. To be effective in the execution of BSA AML compliance requirements, there has to be some level of automation of mass administrative tasks (Meager, 2017) with management rationale and oversight involvement. A totally manual process is not effective, neither is a totally automated process with no human involvement in reasoning and interpretation of outputs effective. Several banks have used some automated technological tool such as blockchains with management involvement successfully. There are banks that have rolled out a partial automation of the BSA AML process. There are banks in India that have onboarded new clients in 2020 using KYC video (Kesanapally & Sikhakolli, 2023). Some large banks have invested in blockchain technology through build-in risk mitigation tools, customer identification, and transaction monitoring activities to deter and prevent money laundering (Campbell-Verduyn, 2018). Blockchain controls activities (AML-compliant registries, identify holders of Crypto currency (CC) wallets in nearly real-time manner, create blacklists of users) designed were proven to be effective in deterring money laundering (Campbell-Verduyn, 2018). However, there are some institutions that have done the opposite of leveraging technology to meet AML regulatory demands; instead, they have opted to take on de-risking strategies that are less costly than technology by refraining from doing business with high-risk individuals/companies/countries that would expose them to penalties. Rose (2020) stated banks in countries such as Denmark implemented de-risking at a national level by terminating clients that exposed them to high transaction costs, high risk, and paused onboarding of all new corporate clients unless they can furnish an external audit report. Rose (2020) continues to say that banks de-risk at regional level includes (client, financial institution, member states, all competent authorities) varying degrees of risk exposure agents. Velez (2020) noted from the Delphi study risk management ratings from the panelist in Round 3 indicated high levels of desirability and feasibility for statement with activities (risk culture, governance and oversight, data quality) that involves tone at the top, management oversight displayed below where six or more consensus votes are displayed in Tables 12.1–12.9 (Velez, 2020).

Table 12.1. Governance Practices on Strong Board 3rd Round Data: Consensus.

| Statement | Ratings | Total Number of Panelist Who Selected Each Ratings |
|---|---|---|
| Statement 23 – Governance practices senior bank managers can implement toward capital regulation that are effective in reducing losses entails strong board and senior management oversight. | | |
| | Highly undesirable: Will have major negative effect. | 0 |
| | Undesirable: Will have a negative effect with little or no positive effect. | 1 |
| | Neither desirable nor undesirable: Will have equal positive and negative effects. | 2 |
| | Desirable: Will have a positive effect with minimum negative effects. | 2 |
| | Highly desirable: Will have a positive effect and little or no negative effect. | 6 |
| | Definitely infeasible: Cannot be implemented (unworkable). | 2 |
| | Probably infeasible: Some indication this cannot be implemented. | 0 |
| | May or may not be feasible: Contradictory evidence this can be implemented. | 1 |

Table 12.1. *(Continued)*

| Statement | Ratings | Total Number of Panelist Who Selected Each Ratings |
|---|---|---|
| | Probably feasible: Some indication this can be implemented. | 3 |
| | Definitely feasible: Can be implemented. | 4 |

Table 12.2. Internal Control Practices on Strong Governance Committee 3rd Round Data: Consensus.

| Statement | Ratings | Total Number of Panelist Who Selected Each Ratings |
|---|---|---|
| Statement 39 – Internal control activities toward capital regulation that can be effective in reducing losses includes strong governance committees. | | |
| | Highly undesirable: Will have major negative effect. | 1 |
| | Undesirable: Will have a negative effect with little or no positive effect. | 0 |
| | Neither desirable nor undesirable: Will have equal positive and negative effects. | 1 |
| | Desirable: Will have a positive effect with minimum negative effects. | 1 |
| | Highly desirable: Will have a positive effect and little or no negative effect. | 6 |

Table 12.2. *(Continued)*

| Statement | Ratings | Total Number of Panelist Who Selected Each Ratings |
|---|---|---|
| | Definitely infeasible: Cannot be implemented (unworkable). | 1 |
| | Probably infeasible: Some indication this cannot be implemented. | 1 |
| | May or may not be feasible: Contradictory evidence this can be implemented. | 2 |
| | Probably feasible: Some indication this can be implemented. | 4 |
| | Definitely feasible: Can be implemented. | 3 |

Table 12.3. Internal Control Practices on Escalation 3rd Round Data: Consensus.

| Statement | Ratings | Total Number of Panelist Who Selected Each Ratings |
|---|---|---|
| Statement 40 – Internal control activities toward capital regulation that can be effective in reducing losses includes reporting and escalation, | | |
| | Highly undesirable: Will have major negative effect. | 0 |
| | Undesirable: Will have a negative effect with little or no positive effect. | 0 |

Table 12.3. *(Continued)*

| Statement | Ratings | Total Number of Panelist Who Selected Each Ratings |
|---|---|---|
| | Neither desirable nor undesirable: Will have equal positive and negative effects. | 1 |
| | Desirable: Will have a positive effect with minimum negative effects. | 2 |
| | Highly desirable: Will have a positive effect and little or no negative effect. | 7 |
| | Definitely infeasible: Cannot be implemented (unworkable). | 0 |
| | Probably infeasible: Some indication this cannot be implemented. | 1 |
| | May or may not be feasible: Contradictory evidence this can be implemented. | 2 |
| | Probably feasible: Some indication this can be implemented. | 4 |
| | Definitely feasible: Can be implemented. | 3 |

The role of the Board of Directors and the importance of their presence in the money laundering risk mitigation efforts are highlighted in their role as key approvers of EWRA. Ghosh (2021) contends an effective compliance function requires the involvement of the Board of Directors and the regulators receiving timely periodic reports based on the reviews of the compliance systems and procedures within the bank. Ghosh (2021) pointed out it is the responsibility of the Board of Directors to oversee the institution compliance function, compliance risk management, and ensure the program is effective. Duncan (2021) mentioned the EWRA methodology document should be approved by the bank's Board of

Table 12.4. Internal Control Practices on Communication 3rd Round Data: Consensus.

| Statement | Ratings | Total Number of Panelist Who Selected Each Ratings |
|---|---|---|
| Statement 41 – Internal control activities toward capital regulation that can be effective in reducing losses includes established expectations for communication and reporting. | | |
| | Highly undesirable: Will have major negative effect. | 0 |
| | Undesirable: Will have a negative effect with little or no positive effect. | 0 |
| | Neither desirable nor undesirable: Will have equal positive and negative effects. | 2 |
| | Desirable: Will have a positive effect with minimum negative effects. | 2 |
| | Highly desirable: Will have a positive effect and little or no negative effect. | 6 |
| | Definitely infeasible: Cannot be implemented (unworkable). | 0 |
| | Probably infeasible: Some indication this cannot be implemented. | 1 |
| | May or may not be feasible: Contradictory evidence this can be implemented. | 1 |

Table 12.4. *(Continued)*

| Statement | Ratings | Total Number of Panelist Who Selected Each Ratings |
| --- | --- | --- |
| | Probably feasible: Some indication this can be implemented. | 5 |
| | Definitely feasible: Can be implemented. | 4 |

Table 12.5. Compliance Practices on Risk and Control Assessment 3rd Round Data: Consensus.

| Statement | Ratings | Total Number of Panelist Who Selected Each Ratings |
| --- | --- | --- |
| Statement 44 – Internal control activities toward capital regulation that can be effective in reducing losses includes periodic risk and controls assessment. | | |
| | Highly undesirable: Will have major negative effect. | 0 |
| | Undesirable: Will have a negative effect with little or no positive effect. | 0 |
| | Neither desirable nor undesirable: Will have equal positive and negative effects. | 2 |
| | Desirable: Will have a positive effect with minimum negative effects. | 4 |
| | Highly desirable: Will have a positive effect and little or no negative effect. | 6 |

*(Continued)*

Table 12.5. *(Continued)*

| Statement | Ratings | Total Number of Panelist Who Selected Each Ratings |
|---|---|---|
| | Definitely infeasible: Cannot be implemented (unworkable). | 1 |
| | Probably infeasible: Some indication this cannot be implemented. | 0 |
| | May or may not be feasible: Contradictory evidence this can be implemented. | 0 |
| | Probably feasible: Some indication this can be implemented. | 2 |
| | Definitely feasible: Can be implemented. | 5 |

Table 12.6. Internal Practices on Three Line of Defense Use 3rd Round Data: Consensus.

| Statement | Ratings | Total Number of Panelist Who Selected Each Ratings |
|---|---|---|
| Statement 46 – Internal control activities toward capital regulation that can be effective in reducing losses includes use of three lines of defense adopting division policies as needed. | | |
| | Highly undesirable: Will have major negative effect. | 0 |
| | Undesirable: Will have a negative effect with little or no positive effect. | 2 |

Table 12.6. *(Continued)*

| Statement | Ratings | Total Number of Panelist Who Selected Each Ratings |
|---|---|---|
| | Neither desirable nor undesirable: Will have equal positive and negative effects. | 6 |
| | Desirable: Will have a positive effect with minimum negative effects. | 2 |
| | Highly desirable: Will have a positive effect and little or no negative effect. | 2 |
| | Definitely infeasible: Cannot be implemented (unworkable). | 0 |
| | Probably infeasible: Some indication this cannot be implemented. | 0 |
| | May or may not be feasible: Contradictory evidence this can be implemented. | 2 |
| | Probably feasible: Some indication this can be implemented. | 4 |
| | Definitely feasible: Can be implemented. | 2 |

Directors, which can minimize biases in the performance of the assessment and increase results credibility. The methodology has four sections: first one sets the tone at the top from Board of Directors toward risk stipulated in their policy statement, highlights importance and commitment, roles and responsibilities of individuals in the execution of a enterprise-wide initiative and cultivation of a risk culture; second section mentions Risk Model core and eight areas in risk assessment/scoring model; third section focuses on administrative reporting line, sanctioning, frequency of EWRA, delegated, approval, methodology maintenance; fourth section considerations for assessors (Duncan, 2021). The EWRA is

Table 12.7. Compliance Practices on Data Source 3rd Round Data: Consensus.

| Statement | Ratings | Total Number of Panelist Who Selected Each Ratings |
|---|---|---|
| Statement 65 – Compliance practices toward capital regulation that can be effective in reducing losses includes clear definition of data source for compliance analytics. | | |
| | Highly undesirable: Will have major negative effect. | 0 |
| | Undesirable: Will have a negative effect with little or no positive effect. | 1 |
| | Neither desirable nor undesirable: Will have equal positive and negative effects. | 0 |
| | Desirable: Will have a positive effect with minimum negative effects. | 2 |
| | Highly desirable: Will have a positive effect and little or no negative effect. | 6 |
| | Definitely infeasible: Cannot be implemented (unworkable). | 1 |
| | Probably infeasible: Some indication this cannot be implemented. | 1 |
| | May or may not be feasible: Contradictory evidence this can be implemented. | 2 |

Table 12.7. *(Continued)*

| Statement | Ratings | Total Number of Panelist Who Selected Each Ratings |
|---|---|---|
| | Probably feasible: Some indication this can be implemented. | 3 |
| | Definitely feasible: Can be implemented. | 4 |

Table 12.8. Compliance Practices on Reporting 3rd Round Data: Consensus.

| Statement | Ratings | Total Number of Panelist Who Selected Each Ratings |
|---|---|---|
| Statement 66 – Compliance practices toward capital regulation that can be effective in reducing losses includes monitoring and reporting activities promptly to upper management. | | |
| | Highly undesirable: Will have major negative effect. | 0 |
| | Undesirable: Will have a negative effect with little or no positive effect. | 0 |
| | Neither desirable nor undesirable: Will have equal positive and negative effects. | 0 |
| | Desirable: Will have a positive effect with minimum negative effects. | 4 |
| | Highly desirable: Will have a positive effect and little or no negative effect. | 6 |

*(Continued)*

Table 12.8. *(Continued)*

| Statement | Ratings | Total Number of Panelist Who Selected Each Ratings |
|---|---|---|
| | Definitely infeasible: Cannot be implemented (unworkable). | 0 |
| | Probably infeasible: Some indication this cannot be implemented. | 0 |
| | May or may not be feasible: Contradictory evidence this can be implemented. | 0 |
| | Probably feasible: Some indication this can be implemented. | 3 |
| | Definitely feasible: Can be implemented. | 7 |

Table 12.9. Compliance Practices Code of Ethics 3rd Round Data: Consensus.

| Statement | Ratings | Total Number of Panelist Who Selected Each Ratings |
|---|---|---|
| Statement 78 – Compliance practices toward capital regulation that can be effective in reducing losses includes top leadership must be a champion of code of ethics. | | |
| | Highly undesirable: Will have major negative effect. | 0 |

Table 12.9. *(Continued)*

| Statement | Ratings | Total Number of Panelist Who Selected Each Ratings |
|---|---|---|
| | Undesirable: Will have a negative effect with little or no positive effect. | 1 |
| | Neither desirable nor undesirable: Will have equal positive and negative effects. | 1 |
| | Desirable: Will have a positive effect with minimum negative effects. | 2 |
| | (Highly desirable: Will have a positive effect and little or no negative effect. | 7 |
| | Definitely infeasible: Cannot be implemented (unworkable). | 2 |
| | Probably infeasible: Some indication this cannot be implemented. | 0 |
| | May or may not be feasible: Contradictory evidence this can be implemented. | 1 |
| | Probably feasible: Some indication this can be implemented. | 4 |
| | Definitely feasible: Can be implemented. | 3 |

a tool used in the effective mitigation of AML which requires banks to develop a full understanding of their exposure to money laundering (Duncan, 2021). The EWRA displays the institution's risk appetite and alignment to the bank's purpose and direction, measurement approach, identification, and handling of risks outside the tolerance level (Duncan, 2021).

The increase in regulatory compliance laws in the United States and around the world has placed stress both financially and operationally on many banks business practices. Global banking regulators have collectively enforced compliance laws to reduce significant bank risks (money laundering, terrorist funding, human trafficking, fraudulent banking activities, bad mortgage loans) that causes significant losses within banks and exposed them to significant penalties and findings. Many banks complained this is overreach of the regulators and a form of over regulation. Regulators deemed these compliance laws and requirements necessary as banks because their locations are plagued with money laundering, funds produced through grand corruption, laundering carried out through complex layering schemes that flows through the banking system as legitimate funds while concealing illegal origins. These money laundering activities conceal sources (drugs, smuggling, gambling, racket, kidnapping, robbery, trafficking women and children) and terrorism, which destabilizes countries and impact their economic stability. The compliance risk exposure these activities pose the global banking sector is one so great it cannot be ignored. Yet many banks fail to implement an effective risk assessment and compliance program. The US government and regulatory sector have taken this risk seriously and have taken actions such as levied sanctions against terrorism-related nations/countries, companies, individuals place them on prohibited list that banks are prohibited from conducting business transactions. Banks found in violation are treated as liability offenses, receive fines, and penalties. Banks are charged with placing teams to monitor and carry out various mitigation measures (cybersecurity, fraud prevention units, BSA/AML management boards, AML intelligence units, AML analysts/ investigators, risk departments, trained network administrators, customer due diligence [CDD]) which are best effective when implemented from the onboarding stage. The consensus statements from the panel of experts relating to compliance when implemented may reduce penalties and findings levied on banks whose compliance programs are found to be ineffective. These consensus statements can help foster effective compliance programs that meet reporting guidelines established in these compliance laws. The panel of experts voting results on maintenance of effective and independent compliance consistent with the organizational objectives, clear definition of data source for compliance analytics, compliance monitoring and reporting activities promptly to upper management, top leadership must be a champion of code of ethics, understanding regulatory compliance when applied as part of the banks compliance framework can yield effective results. Global bank practitioners working in concert with global regulators and various government bodies may use these statements to construct policies, procedures, and training programs that may lead to reduction in global compliance risk that acts as a hindrance to healthy banking sector. These recommendations can help facilitate an effective compliance risk culture that may inform reduction in money laundering and terrorism funding woes that plague the global bank sector.

# References

Abou-El-Sood, H. (2017). Corporate governance structure and capital adequacy: Implications to bank risk taking. *International Journal of Managerial Finance*, *13*(2), 165–185.

Alampalli, S. (2013). Information infrastructure for systemic regulation. *Journal of Financial Regulation and Compliance*, *21*(3), 204–216. https://doi.org/10.1108/JFRC-09-2012-0039

Allen, F., Goldstein, I., Jagtiani, J., & Lang, W. W. (2016). Enhancing prudential standards in financial regulations. *Journal of Financial Services Research*, *49*(2–3), 133–149.

Allison, J. A. (2017). The impact of monetary and regulatory policy on main street banking. *Cato Journal*, *37*(2), 207–215.

Altabet, J. (2022). Transunion v. Ramirez: Levels of generality and originalist analogies. *Harvard Journal of Law & Public Policy*, *45*(3), 1077–1097.

Andrew, E. C. (2021). Is there a commendable regime for combatting money laundering in international business transactions? *Journal of Money Laundering Control*, *24*(1), 163–176.

Baker, C., Cummings, C., & Jagtiani, J. (2017). The impacts of financial regulations: Solvency and liquidity in the post-crisis period. *Journal of Financial Regulation and Compliance*, *25*(3), 253–270.

Baradaran, M. (2014). Regulation by hypothetical. *Vanderbilt Law Review*, *67*(5), 1247–1326.

Barr, M. S. (2017). Financial reform: Making the system safer and fairer. *RSF: The Russell Sage Foundation Journal of the Social Sciences*, *3*(1), 2–18.

Bartlett, R. P., III. (2012). Making banks transparent. *Vanderbilt Law Review*, *65*(2), 291–384.

Bellof, T., & When, C. S. (2018). On the treatment of model risk in the internal capital adequacy assessment process. *Journal of Applied Finance and Banking*, *8*, 1–15.

Berger, A. N., Curti, F., Mihov, A., & Sedunov, J. (2021). Operational risk is more systemic than you think: Evidence from US bank holding companies. *Journal of Banking and Finance*, *143*(2022), 106619.

Bezzina, F., Grima, S., & Mamo, J. (2014). Risk management practices adopted by financial firms in Malta. *Managerial Finance*, *40*, 587–612.

Bieler, S. A. (2022). Peeking into the house of cards: Money laundering, luxury real estate, and the necessity of data verification for the corporate transparency act's beneficial ownership registry. *Fordham Journal of Corporate & Financial Law*, *27*, 193.

Boora, K. K., & Kavita. (2018). Implementation of Basel III norms in banking industry: A review of empirical literature. *IUP Journal of Bank Management*, *17*(3), 7–24.

Campbell-Verduyn, M. (2018). Bitcoin, crypto-coins, and global anti-money laundering governance. *Crime, Law and Social Change, 69*(2), 283–305.

Chang, Y., & Talley, D. A. (2017). Bank risk in a decade of low interest rates. *Journal of Economics and Finance, 41*(3), 505–528.

Chockalingam, A., Dabadghao, S., & Soetekouw, R. (2018). Strategic risk, banks, and Basel III: Estimating economic capital requirements. *The Journal of Risk Finance, 19*(3), 225–246.

Coffee, J. C., Jr. (2018). The retreat from systemic risk regulation: What explains it? (and why it was predictable). *Réalités Industrielles,* 80–90, 115–116.

Crawford, J. (2017). *Lesson unlearned? Regulatory reform and financial stability in the Trump Administration.* Columbia Law Review Online, Forthcoming; UC Hastings Research Paper No. 242.

Croasdale, K., & Stretcher, R. (2011). Community banks: Surviving unprecedented financial reform. *Academy of Banking Studies Journal, 10*(2), 67–85.

Dandapani, K., Lawrence, E. R., & Patterson, F. M. (2017). The effect of holding company affiliation on bank risk and the 2008 financial crisis. *Studies in Economics and Finance, 34*(1), 105–121.

Davies, P. (2015). The fall and rise of debt: Bank capital regulation after the crisis. *European Business Organization Law Review, 16*(3), 491–512.

DeMenno, M. B. (2020). Banking on burden reduction: How the global financial crisis shaped the political economy of banking regulation. *Journal of Banking Regulation, 21*(4), 315–342.

Demetis, D. S., & Angell, I. O. (2006). AML-related technologies: A systemic risk. *Journal of Money Laundering Control, 9*(2), 157–172.

Denev, A., & Mutnikas, Y. (2016). A formalized, integrated and visual approach to stress testing. *Risk Management, 18,* 189–216.

Deos, S., Bullio, O., de Mendonça, A. R. R., & Ribeiro, R. (2015). Banking-system transformations after the crisis and their impacts on regulation. *Journal of European Economic History, 44,* 77–111.

Dowd, K., & Hutchinson, M. (2016). Learning the right lessons from the financial crisis. *Cato Journal, 36*(2), 393–413.

Duncan, P. (2021). A methodology for enterprise-wide risk assessment in small banks and credit union. *Journal of Money Laundering Control, 24*(2), 374–395.

Eastburn, R. W., & Sharland, A. (2017). Risk management and managerial mindset. *The Journal of Risk Finance, 18*(1), 21–47.

Eckert, S. E. (2021). Counterterrorism, sanctions and financial access challenges: Course corrections to safeguard humanitarian action. *International Review of the Red Cross, 103*(916–917), 415–458.

Egly, P. V., Escobari, D., & Johnk, D. W. (2016). The impact of government intervention on the stabilization of domestic financial markets and on U.S. banks' asset composition. *Journal of Economics and Finance, 40*(4), 683–713.

Ehi, E. E. (2021). Identifying and reducing the money laundering risks posed by individuals who have been unknowingly recruited as money rules. *Journal of Money Laundering Control, 24*(1), 201–212.

ElYacoubi, D. (2020). Challenges in customer due diligence for banks in the UAE. *Journal of Money Laundering Control, 23*(2), 527–539.

Erisman, H. M. (2021). Cuba's Roswell connection: A crack in the economic door? *International Journal of Cuban Studies, 13*(2), 331–350.

Fahey, C. (2016). Are we ready for the next financial crisis? *Fordham Journal of Corporate and Financial Law, 21*(2), 232–294.

Fischer, D. (2015). Dodd-Frank's failure to address to address CFTC oversight of self-regulatory organization rulemaking. *Columbia Law Review, 115*(1), 69–125.

Ganegoda, A., & Evans, J. (2013). A scaling model for severity of operational losses using generalized additive models for location scale and shape (GAMLSS). *Annals of Actuarial Science, 7*(1), 61–100.

Gatzert, N., & Schmit, J. (2016). Supporting strategic success through enterprise-wide reputation risk management. *The Journal of Risk Finance, 17*(1), 26–45.

Gerbrands, P., Unger, B., Getzner, M., & Joras, F. (2022). The effect of anti-money laundering policies: An empirical network analysis. *EPJ Data Science, 11*(1), 15.

Ghosh, T. P. (2021). Compliance risk management in Indian banks: Analysis of regulatory actions. *Prajnan, 50*(1), 73–99.

Gladstein, A. (2021). Financial freedom and privacy in the post-cash world. *Cato Journal, 41*(2), 271–293.

Goldberg, M. (2017). Much of model risk does not come from any model. *Journal of Structured Finance, 23*, 32–37.

Hale, B. (2016). The political economy of financial regulation policies following the global crisis. *International Journal of Economics and Financial Issues, 6*(2), 607–616.

Hanke, S. H., & Sekerke, M. (2017). Bank regulation as monetary policy: Lessons from the great recession. *Cato Journal, 37*(2), 385–405.

Helena, H. A., & Madsen, D. Ø. (2021). Developing a maturity model for the compliance function of investment firms: A preliminary case study from Norway. *Administrative Sciences, 11*(4), 109.

Herring, R. J. (2016). Less really can be more: Why simplicity & comparability should be regulatory objectives. *Atlantic Economic Journal, 44*, 33–50.

Hogan, T. L. (2021). A review of the regulatory impact analysis of risk-based capital and related liquidity rules. *Journal of Risk and Financial Management, 14*(1), 24.

Hogan, T. L., & Meredith, N. R. (2016). Risk and risk-based capital of U.S. bank holding companies. *Journal of Regulatory Economics, 49*(1), 86–112. https://doi.org/10.1007/s11149-015-9289-8

Johnson, J., & Desmond Lim, Y. C. (2002). Money laundering: Has the financial action task force made a difference? *Journal of Financial Crime, 10*(1), 7–22.

Kapinos, P., & Mitnik, O. A. (2016). A top-down approach to stress-testing banks. *Journal of Financial Services Research, 49*, 229–264.

Kerimov, A., Koibichuk, V., & Mynenko, S. (2020). Blockchain technology in bank's anti-money laundering. *Economic and social development: Book of proceedings*, pp. 874–883.

Kesanapally, K., & Sikhakolli, S. S. (2023). Optimization of Financial Risk Management (FRM) using Amazon Web Services and Microsoft High Performance Computing at Federal Home Loan Bank, U.S.A. *Phronimos, 3*(1), 71–81.

Lai, K. (2018). HMKA: Regtech is one answer to increase in regulation. *International Financial Law Review*.

Le, H. T. T., Narayanan, R. P., & Van Vo, L. (2016). Has the effect of asset securitization on bank risk taking behavior changed? *Journal of Financial Services Research, 49*(1), 39–64.

Lee, L. (2015). Successfully navigating CCAR and DFAST. *Journal of Structured Finance, 21*(3), 51–55.

Lin, J.-H., Chen, S., & Huang, F.-W. (2018). Bank interest margin, multiple shadow banking activities, and capital regulation. *International Journal of Financial Studies, 6*(3), 63.

Linstone, H. A., & Turoff, M. (Eds.). (1975). *The Delphi method* (pp. 3–12). Addison-Wesley.

Loh, X. (2021). Suspicious activity reports (SARs) regime: Reforming institutional culture. *Journal of Money Laundering Control, 24*(3), 514–524.

Meager, L. (2017). Regtech must serve a purpose. *International Financial Law Review.* https://www.iflr.com/default.aspx

Meral, Y. (2020). Strategic management to prevent money laundering: The role of effective communication. *Journal of Accounting and Finance, 20*(6), 32–48.

Mohamed, A. R. (2015). Effective regulatory regimes: A comparative analysis of GCC financial regulators. *Journal of Financial Regulation and Compliance, 23*(1), 2–17.

Mugarura, N. (2015). The jeopardy of the bank in enforcement of normative anti-money laundering and countering financing of terrorism regimes. *Journal of Money Laundering Control, 18*(3), 352–370.

Panda, B., & Joy, S. (2020). Dynamics of technological evolution in Indian Banking. *Prajnan, 48*(4), 319–343.

Paulet, E. (2016). Regulation and stability of banks in large-scale crises: An historical approach. *Journal of European Economic History, 45*(1), 99–118.

Petitjean, M. (2013). Bank failures and regulation: A critical review. *Journal of Financial Regulation and Compliance, 21*(1), 16–38.

Rathod, M. M. (2022). Operational risk – Business case studies and lessons for banks. *Vinimaya, 42*(3), 5–31.

Rifai, E., & Tisnanta, H. S. (2022). Role of law enforcement to prevent cyber laundering and asset recovery from overseas. *International Journal of Cyber Criminology, 16*(1), 110–122.

Rose, K. J. (2020). De-risking or recontracting – The risk dilemma of EU money laundering regulation. *The Journal of Risk Finance, 21*(4), 445–458.

Sanders, T. B. (2015). The unintended consequences of Basel III: Reducing performance ratios and limiting bank access to equity funding markets. *Quarterly Journal of Finance and Accounting, 53*(1), 97–144.

Seelke, C. R. (2020). Venezuela: Overview of U.S. sanctions. *Current Politics and Economics of South and Central America, 13*(1), 21–27.

Strebel, P., Cording, M., & Shan, J. (2016). Competitive profits and the annual report: Measuring the sustainable business. *Journal of Business Strategy, 37*(2), 42–49.

Sullivan, M. P. (2018). Cuba: U.S. Restrictions on travel and remittances (updated). *Current Politics and Economics of South and Central America, 11*(4), 375–442.

Tanda, A. (2015). The effects of bank regulation on the relationship between capital and risk. *Comparative Economic Studies, 57*(1), 31–54.

Teichmann, F. M., & Falker, M.-C. (2021). Money laundering via underground currency exchange networks. *Journal of Financial Regulation and Compliance, 29*(1), 1–14.

Tsung-Ming, Y. (2017). Governance, risk-taking and default risk during the financial crisis: The evidence of Japanese regional banks. *Corporate Governance, 17*(2), 212–229.

U.S. Government Accountability Office. (2020). Venezuela: Additional tracking could aid treasury's efforts to mitigate any adverse impacts U.S. Sanctions might have on humanitarian assistance*. *Current Politics and Economics of South and Central America, 13*(2), 249–316.

Vahid, M. I., Norton, S. D., Salehi, M., & Moradi, M. (2021). Perception versus reality: Iranian banks and international anti-money laundering expectations. *Journal of Money Laundering Control, 24*(1), 63–76.

Velez, S. (2020). *Banking and effective capital regulation in practice: A leadership perspective.* Routledge.

Velez, S. B. (2022). *Operational risk management in banks and idiosyncratic loss theory: A leadership perspective.* Emerald Publishing Limited.

Walker, D. A., Dammeyer, E., & Lee, E. (2017). Banks' Dodd-Frank costs vs. earnings on reserves. *Journal of Accounting and Finance, 17*, 10–28.

Wall, L. D. (2017). Recent changes in US regulation of large foreign banking organizations. *Journal of Financial Regulation and Compliance, 25*(3), 318–332.

Wan, J. S. (2016). Systematically important asset managers: Perspectives on Dodd-Frank's systemic designation mechanism. *Columbia Law Review, 116*(3), 805–841.

Webb, L. (2004). A survey of money laundering reporting officers and their attitudes towards money laundering regulations. *Journal of Money Laundering Control, 7*(4), 367–375.

Yeh, T.-M. (2017). Governance, risk-taking and default risk during the financial crisis: The evidence of Japanese regional banks. *Corporate Governance, 17*(2), 212–229.

Yeoh, P. (2016). Corporate governance failures and the road to crime. *Journal of Financial Crime, 23*(1), 216–230.

# Index

Printed and bound by CPI Group (UK) Ltd, Croydon, CR0 4YY

10/04/2024

14481720-0005